TWAYNE'S WORLD AUTHORS SERIES

A Survey of the World's Literature

Sylvia E. Bowman, Indiana University

GENERAL EDITOR

FRANCE

Maxwell A. Smith, Guerry Professor of French, Emeritus
The University of Chattanooga
Former Visiting Professor in Modern Languages
The Florida State University

EDITOR

J. M. G. LeClézio

TWAS 426

J. M. G. LeClézio

J. M. G. LeCLÉZIO

By JENNIFER R. WAELTI-WALTERS

University of Victoria

TWAYNE PUBLISHERS

A DIVISION OF G. K. HALL & CO., BOSTON

Library of Congress Cataloging in Publication Data

Waelti-Walters, Jennifer R
    J. M. G. LeClézio.

    (Twayne's world authors series; TWAS 426: France)
    Bibliography: p. 173 - 77
    Includes index.
    1.   LeClézio, Jean Marie Gustave, 1940–   2. Authors,
French—20th century—Biography.
PQ2672.E25Z96   843'.9'14   76–45617
ISBN 0-8057-6266-3

FOR FRANK

Contents

About the Author

Jennifer R. Waelti-Walters received the B. A. Hons. from the University of London in 1964; the Licence-ès-Lettres from the Université de Lille in 1966; and the Ph. D. in French from the University of London in 1968. Dr. Waelti-Walters has been a member of the faculty of the University of Victoria (British Columbia) since 1968. She is currently an Associate Professor of French.

Preface

By the time this volume is published or shortly thereafter J. M. G. LeClézio will have written more books. I have been very conscious of this fact of continued production and development throughout my study of his work from 1963 to 1975 and trust that by drawing attention to major themes, structures, recurrent images, and evolving attitudes within the body of writing I shall have prepared the reader in such a way that all future reading will be more immediately fruitful, and that the inner coherence of LeClézio's books will be recognized and recognizable. This critical study is intended as an introduction to a young author and as a basis on which to build an understanding of his work.

I should like to thank the author for his kind assistance in this project and for his permission to use the poem quoted from *L'Express* and the Canada Council, without whose help the necessary research could not have been accomplished; I am also indebted to Jean-Pierre Mentha, who patiently checked my translations.

I wish to thank also Editions Gallimard for permission to quote pages 136, 137, and 138 from *L'Extase Matérielle* and to Jonathan Cape and Atheneum Publishers for permission to quote translations from LeClézio's work.

NOTE: As this book goes to press, I learn that LeClézio has published his own translation and commentary of ancient Mayan texts. These writings and LeClézio's interest in them reinforce a number of points made in this study.

Chronology

1940   J. M. G. LeClézio born April 13 in Nice.

1940– Family moves about France because of the war.
1947

1947– In Africa where his father is a doctor.
1950

1950– Secondary education in Nice.
1957

1958– In England teaching at Bath Grammar School and as a stu-
1959   dent at Bristol University.

1960– In London as a student. He marries.
1961

1959– A student at the Institut d'études littéraires (now University)
1963   de Nice.

1963   He is awarded a Licence-ès-Lettres in Humanities. This is
the equivalent of a Bachelor of Arts degree.

1963   Publishes *The Interrogation*, which wins the Théophraste
Renaudot Prize.

1964   He receives a Masters' degree from the University of Aix-
en-Provence for his thesis on the "Theme of solitude in the
works of Henri Michaux."

1964   Registers for a doctoral dissertation on Lautréamont.

1965   *Fever*.

1966   *The Flood*. Begins three years of military service. He takes
the teaching option and goes to Thailand to teach at the
Buddhist University of Bangkok.

1967   Publishes *The Ecstasy of Matter* and *Terra Amata*. Goes to
Mexico to teach at the University of Mexico.

1969   *The Book of Flights*. Begins fours years with the Embera
Indians in Panama.

1970   *War*.

1971   *Haï*.

1973   Publishes *Mydriase* and *The Giants*.

1974   Lives in Mexico.

1975   *Journeys to the Other Side*. Returns to Nice.

1976   Publishes *Les Prophéties du Chilam Balam*, translation and
commentary of ancient Mayan texts.

CHAPTER 1

Introduction

AT the time of writing (1975) J. M. G. LeClézio is thirty-five
years old and has already published seven novels, a volume of
short stories, one "nouvelle," and two book-length essays; further-
more, he says that he is working on another essay, more stories, and
a novel—all of which give him some considerable claim to our
notice, especially since his first novel *The Interrogation* (1963) won
instant acclaim and the prestigious Théophraste Renaudot Prize.

As we have seen in the chronology, he has spent long periods of
his life away from cities and civilization; indeed, he looks upon
himself as a man of the forest rather than of the city, even though his
home base is still Nice, where his parents are established. However,
roaming to the remoter areas of the globe seems to run in his family.
The LeClézios are of Breton origin but moved to Mauritius a
number of generations ago; they thus became British by nationality
when the island joined the Empire. Thus it was that J. M. G.
LeClézio's father could be a doctor in the British Army and travel to
the Honduras, Nigeria, etc. during his career—in each instance in
the company of his family.

Since he graduated from high school in Nice at the age of eighteen
LeClézio has continued the habit of traveling himself. First he spent
time in England as a student and then when the time came for his
military service he availed himself of the option of going to some
foreign country as a teacher of French literature. Thus he was able
to live in Thailand for a year while teaching at the Buddhist University of Bangkok. We see influences of Buddhist thought in much of
his later work, particularly in *L'Extase Matérielle* and *The Book of
Flights*.

After a year he was transferred to Mexico where he finished his
military service and the influence of Mexico has been very clear in
all his subsequent writing. We find Mexican gods, rituals and place

13

names used from time to time and above all the concept of the sun as it is used in all LeClézio's work. It is a dangerous force which reinforces man's solitude and even kills while at the same time being necessary to his very life; and this concept came to full development during this period.

Central America offers a much more violent contrast between village life which has remained unchanged for generations and the fast pace of the modern city than can be found in Europe. Faced with such a polarization of possibilities LeClézio left the city altogether after his contract in Mexico had ended and he lived for four years in the forest of Panama with the Embera Indians. He studied their ways and adopted their values to such an extent that he withdrew from publication a book that described his experiences with the Indians because he felt it betrayed what they had taught him. Already since his return to France in 1973 he has returned to Central America several times for prolonged stays and he is presently translating an old Mayan text.

Given this behaviour, which is very like that of his character Young Man Hogan in *The Book of Flights*, it is not surprising that J. M. G. LeClézio should write many of his books in the form of a journey; nor is it strange that he should show a great interest in the biological and geological aspects of the world. For him the world is a mysterious, dangerous, powerful, and wonderful place that man must struggle to understand but from which he is separated by buildings, electricity, technology, cars, words, people—an ever-increasing multitude of man-made objects from which we must escape before we can perceive the aspects of the world which are normally outside the scope of everyday reality. Madness, walking, emotion, drugs, meditation—all can and do serve to break down the barriers that confine our understanding. LeClézio describes them all in such a way that we share every minute particle of his characters' experience: anguish, confusion, and joy. Theirs are the concerns of today: the concerns of people whose world is rapidly deteriorating to a level which it is impossible to tolerate. And they are seeking solutions to this situation.

LeClézio is not writing avant-garde literature in the sense given to it by "litterateurs." He is not concerned with form, with the problems pertaining to the text alone, which isolate literature from the world in which it is created. Hence, he is connected to none of the modern movements in French literature. He stands by himself, expressing his anguish and his quest in powerfully lyric prose which breaks the traditional bounds of the novel and creates an epic of consciousness rather than of deeds. Through him contemporary French literature takes an active part in the definition of the problems of our world. His is an important voice, a voice truly of our time.

CHAPTER 2

The Interrogation

I *Introduction*

*T*he Interrogation is LeClézio's first novel and, as in many first novels, we have the impression that the author has poured on to the page everything that he has been thinking about for a long time. The result is a dense, complex book in which the roots of much of the author's later work are apparent. Themes sketched here will be explored more fully in subsequent fiction so that gradually LeClézio's universe will take shape and the author's place within it will manifest itself clearly. To date, the situation is still very much that of Adam Pollo in *The Interrogation:* the love-hate relationship with the city remains, so does the ambivalence with regard to women. Subsequent heroes follow Adam Pollo's lead in seeking escape from society, from themselves and even from their human state in a variety of ways. Flight, aggression and metamorphosis are the three keys to LeClézio's work; we shall return to them time and time again so, bearing them in mind, let us examine their first manifestations.

II *Résumé*

The Interrogation is the story of a twenty-nine year old man named Adam Pollo who, we are told, does not know whether he has deserted from the army or escaped from an asylum. He is living in an abandoned house near the sea while writing letters in a school notebook to his girlfriend Michèle. He leaves the house occasionally to get food, some of which he steals, but mostly he sits in the sun smoking, playing a pipe, and writing. He has thrown his motorbike into the sea so that everyone will think he is dead and Michèle is the only person who knows where he is.

He goes to the beach and follows a dog to its owner. Another day

16

he follows the dog through the city pretending that he is a dog too. He goes to the zoo and watches the animals, meets Michèle in a café and talks about the night he tried to rape her, then has an argument with a soldier. Michèle comes to visit him; they walk around the headland, watch a big fish, and have intercourse on the rocks near the water.

One day Adam goes to play billiards in the house and kills a rat he finds in the billiard room by throwing billiard balls at it. Afraid that the people who own the house will come back, he tries to imagine ways of living in society without being disturbed—things like having elephantiasis.

He goes walking in the rain and pretends to buy nonexistent records in order to watch the shopgirl look for them. Later he sees a drowned man who has just been pulled out of the water, and there is some conversation about drowning. After this he tries to phone Michèle and spends the whole night searching for her. Then we see snatches of the lives of several different couples and are told about the concept of the world Adam had when he was twelve.

Finally Adam goes out to buy food, sees Michèle with an American, borrows money from her, gets drunk, and has a fight with the American. The next morning police come to the house, but Adam escapes through a window. Once in town he goes to the post office and finds a letter from his mother asking him to return home. Shortly after reading it he begins haranguing people in the street about the state of the world, exposes himself, is chased by police, and finally is taken to a mental hospital. In the last chapter he is questioned by psychiatry students and explains some of his actions.

III *The Title*

As the title is the first element of a book which comes to our notice as a rule, let us consider this one as a key to the contents of the novel. The word interrogation (*procès-verbal*) combines the act of questioning with an implication of imminent judgment. The whole process has also a formality backed by the notion of a social contract; it may be viewed as a confrontation between the representatives of established society. We have four such confrontations in the novel at hand: Adam before the psychiatry student; Adam haranguing the passersby; Adam and the blue bowl; and, very early in the book, his attempt to question Michèle about the results of his attempt to rape her. Finally, there is Adam's text entitled "Interro-

gation concerning a disaster among the ants" (167; G 173);[1] written
when he is drunk and disgusted with the whole of mankind. These
five situations indicate to us various levels of the novel: social criticism (Adam's speech before his imprisonment); psychological
makeup of the protagonist (problems with his father, with sex, and
any social role); the metaphysical considerations brought in by the
equation of men and ants; and, stemming directly from this attitude,
which allows Adam to make such a comparison, as well as from his
name, which is indeed as richly significant as the name of the novel
itself, we discover a network of mythical allusions underlying the
rest of the structure. Hence, we find ourselves faced with the com-
position of life in Western civilization today: social limitations,
psychological attitude, philosophical outlook and religious under-
pinning, all of which are called into question by *The Interrogation*
with which we began—and so we see the novel itself as an indictment of modern city life.

Looking back from the next book *Fever* we find that Adam's
phrase "Interrogation of a disaster among the ants" tells us also that
the book is a study of a fight against madness because in the preface
to *Fever* we find the statement: "I don't have much belief in the
higher feelings. In their place I see an army of insects or ants who
nibble away in all directions. Sometimes these minuscule black ar-
rows meet and the equilibrium of man's reason is destroyed."

Thus we realize the symbolic use of the term ants and Adam
Pollo's interrogation becomes also his self-questioning, a personal
analysis of his mental state.

IV *Social Criticism*

If we look at the social aspect first we see that Adam Pollo is the
French equivalent of an American hippie. He has withdrawn from
society—an action which in itself is sufficient to call into question
the system and conditions which he rejects. He continues to chal-
lenge the status quo, however, by the way he lives and at the end by
an impassioned speech which results in his being condemned in
turn by society itself.

His rejection of society is an extensive one. He refuses all its basic
demands: he is neither clean nor tidy and refuses to own
anything—his house does not belong to him, and he has thrown
away his motorbike. He is dishonest, stealing as much as he buys;

and we are introduced to him just after he has broken into a house. He is not sociable; his refusal to live among others stems from the fact that any contact he makes ends in some form of brutality: rape, argument, fighting. His final act before withdrawing mentally as well as physically is to make manifest his criticism that the world belongs to man and that man has made it in his own monstrous image. This he does in a way intended to shock his fellows into awareness—he makes a public speech and exposes his sexual organs. As a result society rejects him as he has rejected it, and he is locked up. We have, in fact, in Adam Pollo a more self-conscious version of Meursault (from Camus, *The Outsider*), who was also condemned for refusing to conform to social norms.

Pollo rejects city life because it is overcrowded, thus forcing people to live like animals and provoking them to aggressive behaviour. There are a number of parallels drawn between human beings and animals in the novel; Adam's own search for Michèle around the city and his brusque sexual encounters with her are very similar to the episode in which he follows the dog and watches it copulate in the basement of a department store. Similarly his description of the animals at the zoo cage by cage (Chapter F) resembles the presentation of different people in Chapter N. Finally, Adam's situation with respect to society is that of the white rat which allows itself to die when life becomes impossible.

The pattern of relationships develops in a parallel way between Adam and the animals and Adam and society. When he follows the dog he is the dog, just as at the beginning of the novel he is himself. He creates in himself the dog's mode of perception and thus its *mental* world. In order to understand others of any species he needs to desire them, (to become aware of them *physically*)—hence the scene at the zoo with the animals and the old woman and his attempts to use intercourse to create a link with Michèle. As the second has not succeeded in integrating him, so the third stage is marked by aggression, the product of frustration: killing the rat and making a speech, which in both cases reveal vulnerability and make a martyr to the cause.

Adam sets himself up as a social martyr by claiming to be a deserter—thus drawing attention to war as well as to social ills. To reinforce this there is the appearance of a couple of soldiers and an argument about Algeria. (Given that this book was written in the early 1960s the title would then invoke both court-martial and torture—the former reference completed in the interrogation by psychiatrists and the latter by the killing of the rat.)

Another condemnation of man's situation is made by the constant reference to the garbage which surrounds Adam everywhere. The fact that Adam seems to rejoice in this aspect of his state is an expression of his attitude to all mankind—it is his revolt against the overt standards of society and, in his role as Adam-the-first-man, and hence all mankind, a powerful image of the true state of affairs.

V *The Psychological Aspect*

This constant presence of filth and putrifaction incorporated in the image "The earth is blue like an orange" (an image which Adam rejects later for cultural reasons), where the earth becomes the equivalent of a rotting sun, leads us to the major presence which haunts the novel—that of death. Death fascinates Adam. He contemplates at length the ways in which he could be killed, lingers over the body of a drowned man, considers suicide, and, all this time, is supposedly playing dead (since he has thrown his bike unto the sea with the intention of making everyone think he has drowned).

Death tempts him as a final withdrawal from life when other ways fail, because what in fact appears to society as revolt and rejection would really seem to be fear. Adam does not feel capable of dealing with the everyday world and thus tries to escape from it. He leaves home because he is unable to maintain the relationship with his parents which he feels they expect. (He has done this twice.) When he cannot create a deep bond with Michèle, even through sexual contact, he runs away from her. (This happens twice also.) In each case the pattern is the same: a feeling of powerlessness under pressure, aggression, and flight. We see the whole sequence played out in the scenes with Michèle and the American and, on a grander scale, in Adam's rapport with society. He dislikes society because he feels powerless to live as it wants him to do; therefore, he attacks it in his speech and flees to the asylum.

Escape is a major activity in Adam's life. First come physical departures. Each is engineered to appear as though Adam was forced out by circumstance but, in fact, he leaves in order not to face the consequences of something he has previously chosen to do. He claims to have left the army, leaves home, leaves Michèle, runs away from the Bus Station Garden where he had the fight, leaves the house and also the spot where he makes his speech, and at the end is planning to escape from the asylum. In each case he provokes his own entry into the place or situation from which he has to flee—sometimes at some considerable effort.

Adam has other ways of escaping from daily life; one noticeable way is into daydream, but the most frequent and important one is into a state of metamorphosis. Justified by the desire to understand the whole of creation, he tries to enter into different levels of being: pebbles on the beach, lichen and moss, and finally animals. His most successful departure from self is when he follows the dog through the city, his most revelatory when he kills the rat. Both of these identifications are comments on his opinion of himself as less than a human being, while they increase the confusion of his perception of an already diminished sense of self. At the same time they comfort Adam by offering a world in which he is equal to or more powerful than the other elements that surround him. Of this he is quite aware and, indeed, he offers to the psychiatrists an explanation of his behaviour in terms of role inversion between children, plants, and animals—where children take on the power and authority that is wielded over them and become aggressors in their turn. Such an effect would cover the torture of the rat.

Adam escapes when cornered or afraid—at the end of the questioning, after his outburst, he escapes into sleep. Fear is his main feeling throughout the book and he seems powerless to avoid it. (When he leaves society and finds a house he is haunted by the absent owners, etc.) Fear diminishes his sense of self, which in turn impedes the making of appropriate social responses. He thus finds himself constantly in situations where something seems menacing; the result is fear, and the cycle begins once more.

By his own definition Adam has remained in the position of a child in relation to the outside world. He believes that living is accomplished by following certain rules which one should know and that if one knows and abides by these rules then there is a logical result that one can understand and even, in a certain measure, predict. Whenever he creates a universe for himself he constructs it to operate in this perfectly regulated fashion. The real world is beyond his comprehension.

Within the real world he follows sense impulses for only a part of the time (hunger, thirst, sexual desire, fear) and acts upon them.

But he has no moral sense. If he wants chocolate, then stealing it is just as acceptable as buying it, indeed better, for then he shows he has, for the moment, the upper-hand in the game. The same would seem to be his attitude to sex, hence his rape of Michèle. There seems to be no feedback from his experiences to a concept of self; and it is to this that Adam is referring when he accuses the psychiatrists of confusing "existence as lived reality" and "existence as *cogito*" (231; G 236–37).

Although all his responses are disconnected Adam is no fool. Not having been able to escape from society himself he allows it to offer him the protection he needs. The doctor's diagnosis may well be correct; but by labeling Adam as a case rather than understanding him as a person the doctor turns him into an object once more—the whole cycle of minimization is reinforced. However, that would seem to be what Adam wants in order to maintain unharmed his mythic and ludic universes.

VI   *Mythical Resonances*

Our protagonist is called Adam Pollo and comprises within himself by his name the two major streams of influence on the Western world: Judaism—Adam; and Greece—A. Pollo. This he points out in his own musings in the last chapter where he refers to "an alternation of stars of David and suns" (200; G 206). He combines also all the weaknesses of man with the power of a god and, as we have seen in the study of his psychological makeup, this causes him to fluctuate from a feeling of total insignificance to a belief that he is ten feet tall and can accomplish anything he chooses. Apart from this personal element, however, the protagonist's name has importance within the novel because of the symbolic weight it adds to what might otherwise be insignificant detail.

We must remember that Apollo is the god of the sun, of the arts, and of divination and, by extension, is the bringer of madness; for he gives to his initiates knowledge that no one else will take seriously or can understand. Adam sits in the sun and writes letters to Michèle (his notebook which will become the novel), but the malefic influence is clear from the beginning. When he tries to draw the sun he manages to create a black tumorlike octopus which he compares to the intestines of a horse (8; G 17) and which he cajoles like a child: "You're a beauty—beautiful beast, beautiful beast, there, you're a nice sun, you know, a beautiful black sun." This image recurs in the description of the world drawn by Adam when he was twelve, only this time it is a horse with spider's legs which is chasing the only man in the picture across the sky. As the horse is recognized as Apollo's animal, the symbolism is quite obvious. And, of course, once in the mental hospital, Adam is given a room on the north side, "hermetically sealed against the sun" and he is prevented from writing—hence the hospital is there to protect him from Apollo and therefore from madness.

Adam, like Cassandra, tells stories that no one understands; in his final speech in the street he proclaims the downfall of civilization just as Cassandra did that of Troy—with similar fruitlessness. Several times during his wanderings Adam meets an old lady and each one brings him a little more understanding. First there is the lady with varicose veins whom he sees in Prisunic and whose body he wishes to explore further; then there is the lady in the zoo with whom he establishes contact, but she refuses to allow him to learn all he wants to know because it is too late and the sun has gone down; and finally there is the apocalyptic description of the old woman who had made the world.

Suddenly I heard muffled sounds, coming in my direction, I looked down the road, and there, coming into sight slowly, terribly slowly, was an old woman, a fat, ugly old woman, in a flower-printed coat that billowed round her like a flag. First I saw her head, then her shoulders, then her hips, her legs, and finally the whole of her. She was toiling up the tarred road, on her fat, blotchy legs, puffing like a cow, her mind a blank. I watched her emerging from the hill, like getting out of a bath, and coming up towards me. She cut a paltry figure, a black silhouette against the cloudy sky. She was, that's it—she was the only moving thing in the whole region. Nature all round her was unvaried, motionless—except that—how should I put it?—it was making a halo round her head, as though she had the earth and sky for her hair. The town was still stretching away towards the sea, so was the river, the hills were still rounded and the trails of smoke still vertical. *But they extended from her head.* It was as though it had all tipped up. It had altered. It was she, you understand, she who'd made it all. (190; G 196)

Clearly, even without the comparison of the nurse to a medium, these old women are the sibyls of ancient Greece, the oracles of Apollo to whom everyone sent for advice and who provide Adam with his ultimate message.

Apollo's principle form is that of the sun, but we must not forget that he also manifested himself as a dolphin and, although the big fish Adam and Michèle watch swimming round and round in the bay is not given his name, the possibility of a further parallel exists there. Apollo is therefore linked to both the sun and the sea—both bringers of death—and by extension to rocks which are intimately connected to both. The countryside of *The Interrogation* is truly Apollonian, with Adam's house high on the hillside and the sea in the distance reminiscent of a temple.

Adam Pollo's madness links him to Apollo, but his frequent thought that he is the only man alive ties him tightly into a sequence of Judaic and Christian reference, indeed, as does the fish and the dog; for we should note that on his very first excursion it is a black dog that leads Adam to a woman: this dog could well signify the devil, for it is the form in which he appeared to Faust. In this second pattern, Michèle plays two roles—that of woman (Eve) and that of Michael, the archangel whose name she bears. We are told that Adam's first sexual encounter with Michèle was in the forest under a huge tree, and his comment places the action in context immediately: "For me, you understand, you'd become just a heap of pinkish earth, mixed with grass and raindrops" (23; G 33). This event is told early in the novel; from then on Adam is searching for a better understanding of the world, on the edge of which he lives. He does not abide by its rules and so is chased from his Eden—the abandoned house—as a result of Michèle's report to the police.

Young Adam's drawing has resonance in this symbolic sequence also, for the frame of his picture becomes the walls of the garden, the black horse metamorphoses into the symbol of the devil and threatens man with a fall from innocence—which fits easily into the fiction of madness; for with a loss of innocence comes an awareness of the complexity of the world. This brings confusion, a loosened grasp on reality, and a loss of moral sense which would seem to describe the psychological situation of Adam Pollo.

Another of the original Adam's traits is that he is allowed to give names to all things—and this our protagonist profits from fully. Attention being drawn in this way to the names in the novel, we are struck by the Christian ring of many of those borne by the people around the drowned man: *Christ*berg, *Simon*in, *Joseph Jacqu*ineau, *Simone Frère*, *Jean*not and *Paul*.

The original Adam's fall brought death into the world, but our Adam considers himself a martyr for the salvation of mankind—

hence a kind of Christ figure. This recalls the slaughter of the rat—
the scene which is central to Adam Pollo's notebook and in which he
identifies with the rat at the same time as he, Adam, the symbol of
mankind, is killing it. The white rat is the first consenting martyr
and, indeed, when Adam finds it again it has a crown of thorns. (91;
G 98) Hence, in Chapter H we have a symbolic manifestation of the
first Adam's responsibility for the death of Christ, and in Chapter I
we find a similar manifestation for the other Adam, Adam-
Everyman, who finds the dead rat and does not understand its
significance. He has forgotten the whole sequence of events.

The implication of such a description is an indictment of the state
of Christianity in the world today. It also mobilizes extremely powerful symbolism to support the actions of our modern Adam—the
one who can perhaps begin life again with Julienne. (Is it intentional
that she should bear the name of Julian, the emperor who tried to
turn the Roman Empire back from Christianity to paganism?)

LeClézio uses this battery of images sparingly, which is fortunate
or his novel could have been overpowered by them. However, they
add considerable power to his references to God, to creation, and to
catastrophe. One mention which helps to set the final tone is the last
metaphor in which Adam is described as "crucified in limpness and
repose." If we consider this as mockery, in that Adam Pollo is now in
Paradise again, perhaps we have the right perspective on the whole
mythic element in the novel. The psychiatry students little realize
that Adam had a much higher aspiration than that of being Napo-
leon! Adam Pollo is God.

VII *A Ludic Universe*

It is not at all certain whether Adam is playing at being mad or
not—nor is it clear that this aspect of his personality is not an element of his folly. He refers to children, preferring to retreat into a
"ludic universe" where they are on a par with or stronger than the
other elements and where they themselves take on the role of
adults, while forcing animals, plants, etc. into their own weaker
position (215; G 221). (Adam's relationship with the rat and the
exchange of roles there is an excellent example of the pattern described.) Hence, he is aware of the element of role and game, and it
is very possible that he is exploiting it, playing with the psychiatrists
in order to get accepted into a new Paradise. It is indeed a remarkable coincidence that on the very day he receives his mother's letter,

which reminds him of his first fall from grace—the incident of the blue bowl, when his father was angry because he thought his son was mocking his authority—, Adam should decide to flout the values of society (explaining his attitude and exposing himself being two ways of presenting the same intention and vulnerability), and that this should come to the notice of the police. Does it not seem highly probable that Adam set up the rules of this game so that he should be caught?

He is surprised when Julienne gives him the label paranoid. He thinks he should have been classified as a schizophrenic, and the way he expresses surprise leads one to think that this was the role he thought he was playing.

Right from the beginning of the book he is playing dead; then he plays at sex with a human, then in an imaginary game with a lion, a panther, and finally a dog. His letters to Michèle, with possibly one exception, are not real letters, and the records he asks for in Prisunic do not exist. We are told at the end of Chapter J: "He was happy believing in a scale model of the universe, all his own, a gentle place with a thousand different plays [games] to occupy it." (104; G 111) We can trace many of these in the novel. His conversations with Michèle seem to follow set patterns that she recognizes but in which she will not participate. Michèle will not play.

Adam Pollo plays God. In the most elaborate ritual in the novel he kills a white rat by throwing billiard balls at it, and as we have seen in the previous section the rat is a symbol of Christ. While he is killing it he identifies with it, just as children give their role to another and play that of the adult—clearly he is the all-powerful God sacrificing his son. The description of the scene states that the death is necessary because the world is not a fit place for the rat to live in. The killing is formal, and the rat submits to it as the losing player in a game accepts his defeat.

As the first man, Adam, made in God's image, wants to understand the universe in which he finds himself. We have already discussed the drawing he made and the next step is the one outlined as a project of an adolescent friend Sim Tweedsmuir—to reenact the Creation in all its stages in order to comprehend its guiding principles. The important thing is to understand, and the underlying belief is that it is possible to understand, if only for a moment. This explains Adam's outburst against the surrealist image: "The world is blue like an orange"—which does not appear to be a true statement though it follows the rules for a comparative sentence. He is upset when rules he knows produce results which do not coincide with his experience. Everything in life should operate like a game, for in a game the essential element is that it has clearly defined rules which always produce one of a limited number of logically possible solutions. When he is lying on his hospital bed, Adam plans a geometric universe that again has rules and measurements. His explanation of why he cannot bear to live in society is one which fits into this concept of organization toward a solution. Someone broke the rules of reasonable cause and effect and so moved into the absurd world of pure logic, where any result is possible as long as the right formulae are applied correctly to the matter on hand: "Because you made me all wet just now, I'm going to take one of your cigarettes" (239; G 244).

Without rules he cannot continue and so he contrives this very complicated sequence of games which allow him to get to his chosen goal—a place where he becomes a pawn and not a player, where he is told every move to take.

VIII   *Structure and Techniques*

Both ludic and mythic and psychological elements are reinforced by the presentation and organization of material. The chapters are not numbered but rather attributed a letter of the alphabet from A to R. This in itself does not appear significant until we realize that Adam's own story takes us from A to P: Adam Pollo, and that the chapters with extracts from his notebook take us from A to O, a fact which is significantly underlined by Adam's own reference: "Ego Alpha et Omega" (200; G 206). Hence, the notebook contains his "teaching," his "story," just as the Bible does, and at the same time is attributed characteristics of a word game. Q is not used to head the newspaper extract which completes the story of Adam's capture but R could well indicate the medical report made by the psychiatrist.

The story follows that of the original Adam very closely at first, then extends to the state of the modern world. Adam is alone in the house and *garden* (A). A dog (devil) takes him to the *woman* (B). He has *intercourse* with her *under a tree* and then gives her *clothes* to wear. He leaves her (C). There occur many implications of war (D). Adam *understands* the lower orders of life (E), then animals (F). He follows the dog, which goes home into a *garden* to which Adam is

refused entrance (G). Adam kills the rat (that is, he is responsible for
Christ's death) (H). He is then afraid of having to live in society (L).
Then come stories of injustice (J), Awareness of death (K), and other
deaths (L). He searches for Michèle through a modern city and
becomes aware of the sameness of everyone (M). Michèle exhibits
unfaithfulness when Adam's resentment turns around the *coat* he
gave her. He searches for certainty—something fixed (N). There
follows an idea of suicide, fighting, and flight from the house (O).
Adam receives a letter from his mother telling of leaving home. He
accuses mankind (P). After this comes a return to a house and garden where he has no responsibilities and where he makes contact
with a new girl. The structure has turned a full circle, and we are
ready for a new Adam and a new fall.

The weather is used to reinforce the atmosphere of each chapter;
those concerned with depression and death take place in the rain,
the others in sunlight. All violence between humans takes place at
night: the rape of Michèle, the argument with the soldiers, the fight
with the American, and the capture of Adam himself.

The final chapter provides keys to much of what has gone before.
The references to Alpha and Omega and to the two mythologies
have been mentioned already. Manilius and Parmenides provide
alternative fixed systems for understanding the world. The doctor
gives a series of labels which could describe much of Adam Pollo's
behavior earlier in the book, and Adam gives his own explanations.
Here is where the element of play is brought into the open—Adam
refuses the game because the logic of the rules is no longer one he
can understand. This frightens him, and he withdraws in order to be
free to create his own—and that is what he has been doing throughout most of the novel. He has tried to create a world he can live in,
but being unable to do so has forced society to keep him in security
in the center of itself—in an asylum. The house at the beginning of
the novel, the garden in the middle, and the asylum at the end are
one and the same Paradise, where responsibility can be abrogated
and innocence can reign once more. But ahead is another departure:
Adam left his parents' house in secret, left the abandoned house,
and is already planning to leave the asylum even as he appreciates
its tranquility. We are in a spiral of Paradise lost and Paradise re-
gained. The whole sequence seems to be rather a game, especially
when we remember the ever-widening circles of the fish in the bay
and the mirror effects from animal to human in the dog and rat
episodes described above.

One puzzle posed by the structure of the novel is that of the reality of the sequence of events once we have accepted the fiction of Adam Pollo's existence. The sequence of chapters with their days and nights seem quite ordinary until we realize that in C we are told it is August 28, 7:30 P.M. and in O, after some considerable series of events, that it is only 9 A.M. on August 29. Did Adam write things in his notebook in no particular order, or should we believe that Adam invented the whole lot? After all, the doctor does suggest that he is a mythomaniac. Or is it LeClézio this time who is playing with our sense of reality and our security within it?

The author amuses himself a little with the form of the novel, giving us a tongue-in-cheek preface and parodying the well-used formula of the "discovered" notebook by giving us pages with blanks for burned pages, lines crossed out, and typographical errors. We are also given statistics as well as mathematical and chemical notations, but these would seem to suggest another way of understanding and explaining reality, as would the newspaper, and so all of these have a legitimate place in the novel.

The real problem is that of the identity of the narrator. Whoever he is, he writes very easily and moves smoothly from Adam's notebooks to third person narration. There is no change of style for the last chapter, however, as there would certainly be if the last chapter were written from the point of view of the psychiatrist as we suggested earlier. It is a *temptation* to consider that Adam is watching himself write his notebooks and that we have a novel about a novelist writing a novel, but this would seem to be eliminated by the preface and also by the last lines of the book: "While awaiting the worst, the story is over. But wait. You'll see. I (please note that I haven't used that word too often) think that we can count on them. It would be really strange if, one of these days, there were not something more to say about Adam or some other among him" (263; G 248). All we can ascertain are the relationships within the novel:

$$\frac{\text{Mich\`ele}}{\text{Adam}} = \frac{\text{Adam}}{\text{narrator}} = \frac{\text{narrator}}{\text{LeCl\'ezio}}$$

LeClézio is taking us out of the fiction and yet leaving us with a certain possibility of realism—he seems to watch for something to tell us just as Adam does when he goes to town.

The result is a suggested reversal of roles. LeClézio calls his character Adam—the first man he has ever created—and we would like to continue—in his own image. But this is a statement to be treated with some care. Certainly the book is set in Nice, and LeC-

lézio tells us that he found a similar abandoned house when he was
fifteen, at a time when he had a motorbike which he was tempted to
throw into the sea;[2] but the step from there to believing that Adam
is anymore LeClézio than any fictional character is part of its author
is a very big one to take. Perhaps we should remain with Rimbaud's
statement: *je est un autre* ("I is someone else") and apply it to both
the author and his creation.

The novel is, in fact, an attempt to describe consciousness at the
level of the senses where the "I" is the receptor of biological input
and reacts to physiological stimuli such as hunger, sexual desire, and
thirst. The language catches and records minute events as they
occur and does not organize them into either feelings or judgments.
Hence the apparent haphazardness of happenings until we grasp the
mythical substructure. Adam is an itinerant consciousness recording
the outside world as it reveals itself, and the text flows along at the
same level intermingling events, dreams, and passing thoughts in a
lyric style which resembles stream of consciousness writing.

The construction of the book, by the complications it adds to the
story being told (Did it happen or was it a figment of Adam's imagination? Who is "I"? LeClézio? the psychiatrist?), by the reflections
it throws back and forth from person to person, person to animal,
and person to myth, puts the reader in a position with regard to
"reality" similar to that Adam finds himself in with regard to the outside world. In this way we share his feelings to the very end.

IX *Conclusion*

Adam Pollo is the first of a series of heroes who seem to resemble
LeClézio himself in many ways—tall, blond young men, they walk
around Nice or travel around the world struggling to come to terms
with their situation in an environment of hostility, suffering, proliferation, of objects, buildings and even words and death. Pollo gets
the most detailed presentation, the most developed traditional
characterization, the closest analysis. *The Interrogation* is the most
introspective of the novels as, indeed, befits one in which flight from
society takes the form of escape into madness, or at least of refuge
within the physical limitations imposed upon those thought to lack
responsibility or responsiveness to the demands of daily life within a
community. It is a novel of psychological analysis on two obvious
levels and if we take into account the fact that LeClézio says he

writes to maintain his mental balance then we have a third and therapeutic level added.

The problem of coping with the world is one which recurs throughout LeClézio's work. The author offers only two possibilities, as we shall see during the course of this study; these are war and escape. We can wage war against the inhuman aspects of consumer society or we can look for a more congenial place to live. Adam found his other Eden in the mental hospital, other protagonists will choose other solutions: blindness, physical travel, and the changing of mental states and modes of perception, but all of them involve rejection of the modern world as it is depicted by LeClézio—inhuman, vast beyond man's scale, powerful beyond his capability, and yet created by men and imposed by them upon their fellows. This creates distrust, helplessness, and frustration among people, destroying any possibility of relationship between them.

This brings us to the other major theme in LeClézio's work: women. We have seen that Adam's behaviour with Michèle is parallel to his attitude to society: he needs her, violates her, runs away, and still unburdens himself by writing to her. The ambivalence of this first relationship will continue throughout, indeed, it will increase as woman becomes more mysterious, more powerful, and moves from the role of Eve (Michèle) to her incarnation, simultaneously as serpent and goddess in Naja Naja, heroine of *Journeys on the Other Side* (1975).

Thus LeClézio discloses an attitude toward both the individual and society in *The Interrogation*. In the later works a third level will be added to this description: that of humanity's position in the cosmic scheme. *The Interrogation* is the very first glimpse of LeClézio's view of man's estate; and in this novel we can see that this view is a very personal one born, perhaps directly, of the author's response to the demands of his own life. It is certainly true that dealing with city life and women are parallel struggles for the men in LeClézio's books and that these men are set within a frame of philosophical speculation very similar to that LeClézio puts in his essay *Ecstasy of Matter*. As we have said before, they are described in his image, hence they would seem to enter the realm of fictionalized autobiography: Adam Pollo's quest for self-discovery is the first stage of a continuing process.

CHAPTER 3

Fever

I *Introduction*

ONCE again the title, this time of a collection of nine short
stories, offers the key interest which occupies LeClézio and
creates a thematic link among the stories. A fever is something
which can happen to anyone—hence we can all experienc something analogous to what we are about to read—and it has one main
effect: it attacks our normal means of perception, destroying the
limits that mark what we normally accept as reality. During the
course of a fever we see our world move, distort, metamorphose
around us, offering wider possibilities, flashes of apparent and
deeper understanding, different awarenesses. The illness absorbs us
into a consciousness of our body and through it into the material
world of which it is a part. This is the movement which LeClézio
describes in a different way in each of his texts. These are not stories
with the usual kind of plot or twist, though they begin in a similarly
realistic fashion. They do not have a climax; rather, they have a crisis
and a return to the reality of the opening paragraphs. *Fever* is,
therefore, an introduction to the subject matter of the volume and
an indication of the form it will take.

The proximity of fever to madness and the preoccupations outlined above both serve to connect *Fever* with *The Interrogation*. The
texts in the second volume study for themselves, in great detail,
topics and attitudes which were sketched into the earlier novel as
means to a different end; identification with the material universe,
antagonism toward the city, lack of communication, loss of control,
and, of course, death will be offered for scrutiny once more.

II *"Fever"*

Roche Estève goes for a swim, returns home for lunch with his
wife Elizabeth, and has a first wave of fever. Notwithstanding, he

sets off for work but his fever gets worse. He watches a couple making love in a public garden and has a fight with the man as a result; he then throws a brick through the window of the travel agency where he works before running home to bed. Meanwhile Elizabeth is out shopping. Sitting in a café she meets an artist who draws a portrait of her. Roche is hallucinating about Elizabeth to the point where he believes he is a woman. The crisis of his fever over, he feels better and returns to the sea for a swim.

There we have a summary of the main characters' actions—an itinerary of his day and that of his wife. The story itself is, however, concerned with a different kind of journey—one into the body of Roche Estève where all the biological and physiological movement is charted and proves to be the cause which shows its effect in his physical behavior.

As the title indicates we are dealing with the course of a fever produced by sunstroke, but this fever is expressed constantly in images of violence—volcanoes and fire, for example, which find further echoes in human violence. Before his fever starts Roche reads in his newspaper about civil strife in the southern United States and of the murder of an old lady. Under the effect of the fever he gets into a fight and vandalizes his place of work. As a result of the sexual performance he was watching in the park and of his loneliness he has a hallucination about his wife. Sex is linked to violence, violence is linked to death. With his changed perception Roche sees everything as meeting a violent end or moldering to death. The idea of ever-increasing rottenness leads to the idea of dirt, which also has its place in the story.

Roche's fever strips the surface from the world and makes him aware of the corruption around him. It also strips the surface from his behavior and allows his suppressed hatred to explode into action. This perception of reality and hence of values has shifted, allowing him to identify so closely with a woman in his feverish thoughts that at the crisis of fever he feels he has become one himself.

The story turns full circle without coming to any conclusion. Roche goes for another swim at the end, only now he is pursued by a gaze, reminiscent of that of the eye in the tomb which would not leave Cain (in Victor Hugo's *Légende des siècles*). This circular structure encloses, together with the microscopic observation of fever and its results, the statement of a problem which recurs especially in the next story and in the last one, namely, the problem of communication which is encapsulated in the scene between Elizabeth and the artist: the artist does not draw any ears on Elizabeth. LeClézio would seem to be offering his own situation and his problem—his awareness of reality is perhaps different from ours, but he feels that it is impossible to transmit what he experiences. This time the statement is serene but for Beaumont it is a source of acute anguish as we shall see.

III   *"The day Beaumont became acquainted with his pain"*

Beaumont wakes up at 3:25 A.M., cannot get back to sleep, and discovers he has a toothache. The pain gets worse and worse despite aspirins, etc. He becomes afraid of the apartment and so phones his girlfriend Paule. She refuses to come and see him at that hour. His pain gets still worse and he drinks a whole bottle of plum brandy, then starts phoning any number he fancies in order to talk to people. By morning he is absorbed in his suffering; he climbs out on to the roof and contemplates the street.

Within the story we have a constant building of tension, by the violence of the imagery, until the full extent of Beaumont's pain-madness is reached. At first he is merely sensitive to stimuli from outside his body but then he has a strange feeling:

. . . his brain, in some strange way, had turned into a funny kind of animal, a worm, for instance, and the animal was turning round on itself, searching for some unknown thing. The cold creature would crawl imperceptibly forward, then stop short and slowly twist its squat body so as to look behind it. No eyes, but something resembling antennae, or snail's horns, rose placidly out of the cartilaginous mass and, very softly, touched the wall of the skull, the object covered with pink meninges. Beaumont suddenly realized that this fluffy worm writhing inside his head was his brain, his intelligence, himself; whereupon he felt himself invaded by an unfamiliar fear, a precarious, shameful sentiment which he would probably not confess to anybody. (58; G 62)

From this moment on his perception is distorted by pain: "When he had finished he perceived that it was high time, for it had already become impossible for him to read any more. In his head, buried under the red membranes of the meninges, the fat, restless worm had writhed over the last line on the yellow sheet of paper and was spending its time counting the dots, feeling them one by one with its opaque suckers and its soft antennae. It was counting them over and over, tirelessly . . ." (60–61; G 64). Beaumont becomes intensely conscious of his mind, his skin, his fear, but instead of transforming this sensitivity into violent action, as did Roche, he turns in upon himself: "And Beaumont . . . could already feel that the gates of an unknown tragic world were opening to admit him, the gates of a world where disquiet is a form of beauty, an exasperated landscape haunted by memories of the other land, the peaceful, prosperous land where the animals are clear-eyed and the nerves repose in watery silence. Already he could feel the monotonous sadness of the journey . . ." (63; G 66). And once he has accomplished the journey, he finds a new home: his jaw: ". . . he had made his smarting jaw into a shell, an immense, well-proportioned habitation" (65; G 68). But within this house remains the fear which began with the awareness of the worm in his head—a fear of death which has two aspects: that of being alone and that of being killed. The fear sharpens and distorts his perceptions even further, until he sees his pain as a thread which links his body to the matter which surrounds him:

With this new, unforeseen organ growing inside and outside himself, Beaumont was receiving the indication of his own death: stone and plaster, paper, textiles and glass were being cunningly shown to him, he was making their acquaintance, he was being pushed towards them, towards the inhuman calm, the mysterious order where time has ceased to flow, where movement is imperceptible and sensation eternal. That skirting board was himself, so was this rubbish. . . . (72; G 75)

To conquer all this suffering he begins to drink and so increases his vulnerability to altered states of consciousness; with the result that he retreats even further into his pain, until he has the illusion that he is inside his tooth—protected and immortal. The alcohol has taken him over the threshold of his fear, and the previous images come together to express his final state: the worm of his nervous system has coped with the crisis. "Beaumont, sitting in his tooth, nice and warm, nice and uncomfortable, both legs wedged into the grooves of the roots, was swept away by another movement; that of the memory of the sun, for instance, or of being short of time. In the center of his multiform song there was a kind of special animal, an undying worm with feet" (83–84; G 85). So we leave him, his pain unresolved but serenity restored, about to return to the edge of the real world—to the roof where he will sit in the sunshine amidst the excrement of birds.

Throughout his torment Beaumont has constantly tried to describe his situation to others. What they understand has never the poignancy of what he is experiencing, so that the story presents us also with a representation of the problem of communication. With this in mind it would be possible to consider "The day Beaumont became acquainted with his pain" as a description of the situation of an author who has an anguish, a problem which he must share and who feels himself enclosed in a solitude from which he can never escape. Because of the incomprehension of everyone around him, he is then forced to come to terms with his sensitivity and to journey to a place in the outside world where there are no people.

Beaumont would, in this case, be duplicating the action of Adam Pollo and, indeed, the action of LeClézio himself when he leaves city life to avoid the throng. Is the story a prolonged metaphor of LeClézio's own state of mind? Such a case can certainly be made.

IV   *"It seems to me the boat is heading for the island"*

The narrator goes for a walk because he is cold. The story thus begins with an imaginary walk in from the suburbs and then turns into a real one. The narrator walks round one block six times to study it, climbs under and over cars in a huge parking lot, and meets a little girl, then a friend. Finally he lies in the dry riverbed—and disappears.

V   *"Backwards"*

The narrator is shaking as though in a train. He has the feeling that he is shrinking and that someone is gradually taking away part of his name. Someone is also counting backward. He is very aware of his body and of the passing images.

VI   *"The walking man"*

J-F Paoli gets up with a headache as a result of sleeping pills taken because his girlfriend has left him. While he is having breakfast the rhythm of water dripping begins to irritate him, so he goes out and walks all day, losing himself into various objects, becoming afraid of the crowd, gaining a sense of infinity. Finally, a girl's face puts him in harmony with everything and suddenly he can create the rhythm of the morning.

VII   *"Then I shall be able to find peace and slumber"*

The narrator is lying in bed listening to street noises, etc. Suddenly it is as though the concept of day and night had turned inside out. All is bright in his room, then darkens progressively as images pass before him. Something grasps his brain. He fights with an old man and then has a vision of the perennial nature of matter. He desires control.

The four stories outlined above continue the idea of an itinerary of involuntary exploration of modes of perception. In each case there is one character only; three of the texts are in the first person, so that we know that the character is conscious of the changes described at the time when he experiences them. This is not necessarily the case in the other stories. In each case the character is taken out of himself by his physical state. None of these states are as violent as the ones discussed previously, but they serve nonetheless to produce a distorted view of reality and the characters' place within it. In every instance the character is absorbed into the matter around him in some way which serves to heighten and release his emotional state, thus moving him toward a sense of harmony with the universe.

VIII   *"Martin"*

Martin Torjmann is twelve years old and a hydrocephalic genius. He is at least six years ahead in his school exams, wins television quizzes, and gives lectures. He gives a press conference about knowledge and the nature of religious faith as a state of trance similar to intoxication, with a similar void at the peak of ecstasy. One day he goes into the courtyard of the building he lives in and as a result of the movement of sand in the sandpit begins to meditate on life. Later, hailed as a religious leader by the outside world he returns to the sand-pit where he is set upon by a gang of children who torment him. He takes this as divine punishment for blasphemy.

Martin's experience is the reverse of that of the other characters in this collection of stories. While all the others learn to experience the pulsating life of matter around them, Martin is not only aware of the experience but can define it totally. He must escape from his intellectual knowledge into the experience of human emotion. The intellectuality of the boy is important, however, not only to show a variation on the other stories but also to enable the author to bring together in an explicit way the major preoccupations of the entire volume. The opening description of a low-cost housing development is a condemnation of city life; the character, opinions, and situation of Martin is a triple condemnation of the attitude to knowledge today; and the description of Martin and his parents is an illustration of the generation gap. But the most important part of the text, Martin's forced awareness of his human frailty aside, is his presentation and analysis of the state of trance, which is, after all, the state into which all the characters in the book slide in one way or another. "Faith is a trance, and everything approximating to that trance partakes of faith" (149; G 147), says Martin, and he continues:

The state of trance comes almost naturally to a human being; very little is needed to induce it. A trifle, a little alcohol in the bloodstream, a small dose of a drug, an excess of oxygen, anger, fatigue [and here we have a list of the basic premises of the various stories]. But the state is interesting only in so far as it can be guided. It's a loss of balance, but an unbalance that brings unknown regions of the mind into play. In actual fact there is no fundamental difference between a man intoxicated with alcohol and a saint gathered up into ecstasy. And yet there is a difference; the difference of interpretation. The moment of madness is preceded by a phase during which the subject's consciousness is tottering, as it were; he is undergoing a violent cerebral stimulus. That is the phase that really manufactures the ecstasy and gives it meaning. Whereas ecstasy in itself is blind. It is a total vacuum, with no ascent and no fall. A flat calm. So one might argue that the saint will never know God. He approaches Him, and then draws away from Him. And these two stages are the ones that exist. Between them is nothingness. The void, total amnesia. At the moment X of ecstasy, the saint and the drunkard are alike, they are at the same point. They dwell in the same empty, terrifying paradise. (149–50; G 147)

We have quoted this passage in its entirety because it shows the structure of every story in *Fever* and explains the author's interest in the kind of subject treated. Every ecstasy of this kind is produced in a different way, reveals a different vision. The author is describing for us the various ways of achieving a state of trance and the effects each may have. The paragraph above also brings into consideration a mysticism attached to this kind of awareness of the world—which is perhaps responsible for the lyric quality of LeClézio's writing at times. He is offering an escape from the technological world of the opening paragraphs of "Martin" into the beauties of the biological universe.

IX *"The world is alive"*

This is a minute, inch by inch description of countryside as precise as the most detailed map could possibly be. It deals with mountains' shapes and microscopic details in a high valley and then down beside the sea. The description fills out the concept of matter which has recurred in the other stories; following Martin's interest in the sand and Beaumont's idea of death as absorption into changeless matter, it leads us to the final story of the collection.

X *"A day of old age"*

Maria Vanoni has been found lying on the kitchen floor by Joseph the boy who does her shopping. She is on the verge of death and the boy sits watching, questioning, and reassuring her, trying to understand. She is absorbed in herself and has a vision of Jesus, Martha, and Mary with whom she is singing. There is silence. Joseph goes out and walks and walks; absorbed by his picture of the old lady, he is trying to understand. The town increases his feeling of helplessness. He almost commits suicide in the sea, then under a truck to find an answer. Finally he returns to Maria and questions her again.

Like most of the other stories this one comes full circle to an ending which is in no way a solution to the problem posed. Joseph wants to help the old lady and he also needs to understand her death to such an extent that he is absorbed into her:

Perhaps he was no longer himself now. . . . Bound to the moving features of one single old woman, impotent as she was—linked to her glassy, melancholy gaze, stripped of all strength by the memory of her lagging muscles and flaccid skin, treacherously invaded by the whole of that derelict body, in cold and dizziness and silence, Joseph was, so to speak, being lived by her. He was living like a picture, something in the nature of a damp reflection, exposed every second to annihilation and evaporation. (224–25; G 217)

It is at this moment that we learn Joseph's surname: Charon— the name of the ferryman across the river of death. All his actions take on a new importance. This symbolic element occurs again in the tale of the little girl and her cat which runs parallel to the situation in the main text. Joseph and the young Maria regard the old Maria and the cat in the same way, and just as the cat tried to bite the child so Maria believes Joseph has come to do her harm.

Maria Vanoni and the area in which she lives are described with great realism—bringing death clearly into the midst of life in a way that cannot be avoided. The fear that has haunted the whole volume of *Fever* is brought into focus and studied, only to reveal its profound mystery. All we know is that death is cold. Maria can transmit no more.

XI   *Structure of the Volume*

The order in which the stories occur is not insignificant. It reflects an overall movement from life to death, with increased awareness at every stage along the way.

First Roche Estève encounters physical discomfort—a fever. He struggles against it and as he is healthy he has no awareness of anything except solitude. To counteract this he has an hallucination of his wife.

Beaumont feels greater pain, hence his feeling of solitude cannot be palliated by hallucination, nor by speech; and no other contact is available to him. His loneliness turns to paranoia and violent fear. He is then absorbed into his suffering and rejects other people. Roche's pain is in him but Beaumont *is* his pain. The two stories therefore fit together, the one as a logical development of the other.

Physical discomfort of the above-mentioned kind does not happen every day, so the emphasis shifts now to a more ordinary way of achieving a shift of perception: walking for a long time. "It seems to me the boat is heading for the island" and "The walking man" both deal with the hallucinatory effect of constant motion. Again there is a development from one to the other: the narrator of "It seems to me the boat is heading for the island" sets off because he is cold, whereas J-F Paoli is trying to escape an emotional pain.

Between these two stories comes "Backwards," which reminds us of the fever theme and seems to have been constructed especially to occupy its position linking the walking stories in the volume as it opens: "Today, April fifteenth in the year XXV after my birth. Before that walk" and ends "And then, right ahead towards the species of death." "Backwards" has its complement in another story about sleep, "Then I shall be able to find peace and slumber," where there is an increase not only in awareness but in desire to understand, to have control over the shifting images. And this situation leads easily into the subject of "A day of old age."

"Martin" is linked to the story following it, "The world is alive," by the direct interest manifested in the movement of matter, in the physical makeup of the world, and to the story preceding it ("The walking man") by the fear of other people expressed in it. By the concern with God it joins the last story directly. Martin's experience and anguish also act as a pivot between the intense humanness of Beaumont and that of Maria Vanoni, the old woman about to die.

Hence a schema of the links described would look something like this:

Fever
The day that Beaumont became acquainted with his pain
It seems to me that the boat is heading for the island
Backwards
The walking man
Martin
The world is alive
Then I shall be able to find peace and slumber
A day of old age

The texts are in pairs and concern physical discomfort and psychic discomfort, and physical activity and nonactivity (walking and sleeping). Fever leads to insomnia and dreaming by the similarity of the images. Roche's feverish walk leads to the effect of the other walks. The hallucinatory explorations of the world lead to Martin's conscious exploration and to the detailed botanical and biological description of "The world is alive," while the suffering, questioning people are all joined in death to the matter of the universe—a death we join Joseph Charon in trying to understand.

Other links are forged between the various texts by the images which are most prevalent: heat, cold, shrinking, aggrandizement, eyes, insects, and so on. Heat goes together with violence, cold tends to be joined with fear. Everywhere there is constant movement: crowds of cats and people, spots before the eyes, ants, molecules, leaves, dust—every microscopic change is registered in all the texts.

The overall movement is a downward one.[1] The characters leave home, which is usually an apartment, and go down into the street. They move from the suburbs to the center of the city and on to the beach, from the mountains to the sea.

This is, of course, a natural movement in Nice because of its

geographical situation, and it is certainly safe to assert that all these
stories are set in Nice and the surrounding countryside. However,
this movement is symbolic, since each character moves out from his
own individual view of the world, becomes aware of the seething life
around him, and moves through it, studying as he goes, until he
achieves a sense of infinity—the sea or the desert. And at the same
time he moves down to death.

Three worlds are parallel: the body, the city, the natural world.
They are explored with equally minute realism, and are discovered
to have similar structure. Hence, they are mutually enlightening
and symbolically interchangeable. A consciousness seeks its cosmic
counterpart just as a person studies a crowd. The living world is a
hive of activity in the same way as a human body. Our matter,
normally enclosed within itself, becomes permeable to the matter
outside under certain circumstances. The texts of *Fever* describe
some of those circumstances to us, show us the contact that can be
achieved.

Martin Torjmann and Maria Vanoni call it God—and these two
stories are the culmination of the volume. In an interview with
Pierre Lhoste[2] much later, LeClézio will clarify this statement by
saying: "God in infinity, psychoanalytic infinity as well as the infinity
of drugs. *It is that kind of opening that every being has in himself*
and which makes him search, change his place, write, open doors
even if he closes them again immediately."

XII   *Composition of the Stories*

The movement is therefore from awareness of self to an opening
on to the infinite. In each of these stories, if only for a second, the
character is taken out of himself.

The way this shift is effected varies very little from story to story.
We see the character at home behaving normally when whatever it
is that will upset the senses strikes, and we follow the "fever"
through its various stages until the character concerned emerges
once again into the light of "normal" reality. The story is a minutely
detailed written report of the progress of the "sickness," with all its
physical symptoms and mental distortions. As we have seen in the
studies of the individual texts, the "fever" rises in waves, producing
extreme reactions both within the body of the victim and also in his
attitude to the world around him. There is usually an emotional
crisis which resolves itself in action—in violent action—previous to

the physical crisis which is simultaneous with a secondary action. Beaumont's telephone calls and Charon's near suicides would be examples of this, as are Roche Estève's vandalism and sexual hallucination. (These "actions" can, of course, be bursts of imagery.)

The shorter stories are limited to an "interrogation" of a short period of time. The longer ones need a more substantial structure, which is given by the injection at regular intervals of doses of the outside world into the main fantasmagoria—examples are Beaumont's telephone calls and Joseph Charon's conversations with the old lady. "Fever" itself, a longer story, has a whole section devoted to another, a nonfeverish character, Elizabeth, in order to throw into high relief Roche Estève's unusual perceptions and reactions; and the whole of the first part of "Martin" is a long buildup which will serve as contrast to his fear.

Because of the nature of the subject matter the texts have one main character through whom everything is filtered. (Surprisingly only the three shortest stories are recounted in the first person and "The world is alive" is narrated in direct reporting style appropriate to an objective observer. The other stories are told by a traditionally all-seeing author who notices every flicker of consciousness.) He—for they are all male—usually has a friendly female counterpart (Elizabeth, Paule, Germaine, Mme. Torjmann, Maria) who is never as helpful as the protagonist expects her to be in the face of his solitude. Also, he is surrounded by a crowd whom he feels to be antagonistic. The crowd watches him, and he is afraid and/or hates everybody.

This watchful gaze which is turned on the protagonist from outside is a malevolent force which recurs in LeClézio's work, posing a problem to the author himself: "Indeed I find that there is nothing more wearing than the eyes of others who drain you of your substance."[3]

All of the characters are ordinary young men or adolescents. For different reasons they are solitary people who do not identify with the crowd around them even when they are able to fit into the larger pattern of the material world. Thus their "fever" is often born of their sense of alienation transposed in some cases into a physical ailment. Seeing Roche Estève's violent hatred of his office, we wonder whether it has not occasioned his sunstroke in order to provide itself with an outlet. His fever then becomes a means to shed responsibility by escaping from reality—just as Paoli's walk is an obvi-

ous attempt to escape the thoughts of Jeanne. The shift into changed
perception and greater experience is involuntary in the early texts.
Martin is the first character to search for an awareness and understanding of infinity in full consciousness of his actions. (He has to
come upon humanness instead.)

LeClézio, in an interview with Georges Bortoli[4] given while
Fever was being written, substantiates this interpretation and takes
it to the end we have discussed above:

> I am very interested in physical manifestations of passion. We say, love,
> hatred. But that shows itself first in a bodily disorder: a headache, fever, or
> something like that. All these little phenomena join together to make some-
> thing bigger and more mysterious. Hence, we sometimes speak of madness
> and we lock men up for that. At other times we simply say: "He's not well,
> he has a migraine, he's angry."
>
> My characters are excessive. I can't help it. They impose themselves on
> me in this way. At the end of their paltry adventure, after the shock of pain,
> once they are well and truly dazed, they can't help but notice, for a few
> seconds, that they belong to life. They become capable of projecting them-
> selves into the things around them, even into an animal or insect. Because
> we live in others, we project ourselves into others. . . .

There we have the intention expressed in *Fever* and in *The Interrogation* as well. It remains to be seen whether later works continue
this theme.

CHAPTER 4

The Flood

The Flood is both a continuation and a complement of *The Interrogation*. François Besson and Adam Pollo are both tall, thin, neurotic young men who, when they are not walking obsessively around the city, remain as motionless as possible. The heroes are similar; and the city is the same, although this time we find it, not in the despotic grasp of the summer sun but, at the other violent peak of the year—the end of winter, when storms and high tides hold sway. The atmosphere of *The Flood* is, accordingly, diametrically opposed to that of *The Interrogation*. It remains to be seen where the other links between the novels lie.

I *Résumé*

François Besson has a vision of a young girl swallowed up by the sound of a siren. From then on he sees death everywhere in life. A friend sends him a tape on which she explains her own possible suicide. After hearing this, Besson, in a thirteen day pilgrimage, strips himself of all the life around him (people), then of most elements of his own life (food, home, past), and finally of his sight, so that he is irretrievably cut off from the world and immured within himself. At this point he listens to a tape on which his friend has recorded her last moments of life.

II *Structure*

The book is put together like a set of Chinese boxes, and the résumé has concerned itself mainly with the innermost box—the thirteen day picaresque journey (right down to the chapter headings) of François Besson, in which he moves from extreme perspicacity (he sees death in everything) to willful blindness. Thus we have again as the main theme of the novel the story of a flight from awareness.

45

This flight is encompassed by second flight, in the story of Anna, which is recounted in the first and last chapters of Besson's odyssey. Anna chooses to escape a world which she cannot bear by committing suicide; and as she dies she records her reasons on a tape to be delivered to François. Around both of these escapes is placed an evocation of what is being avoided: the flood, the apocalypse, the world working toward its end. There are three separate sections of the novel which indicate three levels of protest, three cries of distress, as we shall see later.

The central section of the novel contains thirteen chapters in which François Besson comes to terms with himself. He strips himself bit by bit of everything that ties him to the earth—even his perception of it. First he is alone with a tape which in some ways describes his own situation to him. The next day he avoids people until he finds an alternative to his own situation—the madman. Following that he fails to come to any understanding with his fiancée Josette and moves away from her. The next possibility offered is the blind man. After these solutions to his problem with the world there is a pause for reflection (in his room). The next possibility offered is Marthe and it seems for awhile that all will be well, but we find him back in his room. Human love has now been rejected three times (his mother, Josette, Marthe).

Next come physical privations—hunger, thirst, cold, no cigarettes—which bring him to try God as a solution. He rejects Him too. François tries work and the friendship of men but being homeless and afraid he kills someone and leaves the town (the human race), finally reducing himself to a minimum by maiming himself physically in such a way that the maximum of contact with others and information about his surroundings are avoided.

The central section, François Besson's experiences, has an obvious structure—that of thirteen successive days. Within these is an irregular structure of patterns of recurrence which both reveal Besson's preoccupations and help the reader to orientate himself within movements which are not chronological.

In every fourth chapter François spends a considerable time in his room. It is there that he learns of Anna's impending and then imminent death; there too he tries to write, reads what he has written as a child, burns his papers in order to rid himself of his past (and in the process almost destroys the room itself). Yet it is to his room that he returns when he has burned out his eyes. He has destroyed not only his attempted communication but his major means of acquiring things to communicate. He has tried to burn his sanctum, the place where he had the greatest possibility of contact with other people, and his eyes by which he made this contact. He is alone in the blackness after the conflagration. This situation links the central sections of the book with the opening and closing sections, where we witness the explosion of the Apocalypse and which in turn reminds us of the explosion François hears in the city early in the book. There is a great difference between the fire François lights and the workmen's and the tramps' fires lit for comfort, warmth, and camaraderie.

In contrast to the element fire is that of water, which takes three forms: rain, river, and sea. The weather reflects Besson's state of mind and his possibilities of emerging victorious from the trials he is undergoing. Hence the constant rain in the first part of the book supports his depression when he is alone and deepens to darkness and rain when he is with Josette. Not until he moves in with Marthe does the sun shine, indicating very clearly the possibility that Besson may find a solution to his misery. The storm is his turmoil as he struggles with his fear of a close relationship with a woman; and the next morning, when he leaves Marthe, the weather is trying to improve but does not manage to do so. The next days are cold and grey, then rainy once more. Finally, when François finds his answer, the sun is high in the sky. After that the weather has no function in the novel, because the problem of how to survive in the world no longer exists in the same form. Death and darkness close in together.

A further shape is given to the thirteen day peregrination by the stories which punctuate François' movements. First there is Anna's story of the snail who is cut off from the world. By the end of the twelfth day we are well aware that this is an allegory of François' life, because he is holding a snail-shaped stone when he sacrifices his sight. The next story is François' justification of his actions—the story of the philosopher who strips himself of everything he has. (The problem is that Besson emulates him not to find the truth but rather to hide from it.) After that come a series of wish fulfillment dreams of indestructible heroes (quite the opposite of François Besson himself): Oradi noir, Texas Jack, Lucas in his own dreams—and we may assume Besson in his as a child—and finally the tale of a real live man, Siljelcoviva the Yugoslav. This is not the kind of hero Besson is destined to be.

III *Themes*

The stories are in direct contrast to the major themes that run through the novel: fear, eyes, and death. Because François sees death everywhere, he is afraid of seeing. Simultaneously, he is afraid of being watched. He rejects emotional contact with people—a contact made through the eyes. Note the scene with his mother: "Eyes, hands, mouth, grey hair—all carried the same message of compassion and love. Besson lowered his head and looked away" (71; G 71); and again with Marthe: "Her great staring eyes blurred, became patches of brown mist, floated towards one another, suddenly merged in the middle of her forehead, forming a moist circle within the unfocused framework of the mask, a circle charged with humiliation and hope. Furiously he plunged into it, no longer hearing the fragmentary words that reached him, calling him by name; plummeted down into the troubled waters of dissension and unhappiness, let them close above his head" (174; G 166). François Besson is haunted by eyes that see through him as he sees through the people who are looking at him—for example, the old women when he is begging. If we take one chapter as a further example we see that he, and hence the novel, is kept in motion by looks which come from different directions. In Chapter 2 he goes to the newsstand to escape the eyes of the crowd, leaves the stand to escape the saleswoman, and goes to a café where he actually takes a dirty glass from another table in order to avoid contact with the waiter. Finally, he is absorbed into an identification with a mentally subnormal young man on a bus, leans forward gazing at him, and frightens him in his turn.

Throughout the novel, eyes produce and witness violence, misery, and death. Hence it is a natural development of this motivating force that Besson should put out his eyes to protect himself from an awareness of all of these things. (The Braille newspaper does not contain such news.) Irony lies in the fact that the most personal death of all comes to him through his ears—he hears the glass fall from Anna's hand after she has said that being blind might have reconciled her to the world.

Death, she says, is like a flood—a flood of water like the storm.

The only person who knows the flood is threatening is the blind man. Will François Besson hear death now? Certainly we are plunged into a whirl of apocalyptic imagery in the last section, just as we were in the first section, before the arrival of the girl on the motorized bicycle. And the opening and closing sections are Besson's perceptions.

In this context we remember how much the novel is, indeed, dominated by noise. There are explosions, car crashes, planes flying overhead, people talking, quarreling, insulting each other, men at work. The traffic roars through the streets while the flood growls along beneath them. We hear the wind and rain as much as we see them—especially in the storm which is a masterpiece of description—and François' parents hear the fire in his room. Above all, of course, we hear the siren which absorbs the girl into itself and kills her for François as it dies; and we hear Anna's tape with the sound of the breaking glass which indicates her death.

This absorption of human life into that of matter takes us into a whole realm of experience expressed both by much of the imagery in the novel and by Besson's identification with a house, a glass, and so on, an absorption which is similar to the metamorphosis we have seen in the previous works. Natural phenomena are often described anthropomorphically: "la mer écarte et renferme ses gencives édentées" (the sea opens and closes its toothless gums)—human experiences and objects have cosmic metaphors; with the result that, to quote Robert Kanters' review in *Le Figaro Littéraire*, "Chaque monde appelle l'autre à son aide pour exister dans notre imagination." (Each world calls the other to help each one exist in our imagination)[1] Human, animal, vegetable, and mineral kingdoms are inextricably mixed with the elements as a result. Herein lies the complexity of the universe, the confusion that François Besson shares with Adam Pollo and the protagonists of *Fever* and which almost seems to be a personal philosophy of J. M. G. LeClézio.

IV *Mankind's Dance of Death: universal awareness*

The novel opens and closes on an image of war linked with a quality of immobility and desertedness that lead inevitably to the idea of death through François Besson's vision of the girl on a motorcycle. The final phrases sum it all up: ". . . and then, hundreds of yards, perhaps miles away . . . the sound of a warning siren, the reverberations of war: like a cat miaowing . . . all alone

on a vast and dreary expanse of tin roof" (300; G 283). At one and the
same time this, the modern city, is man's creation and his downfall.
The environment has been organized to a point beyond the reach of
humanity:

Any part of the view—as it might be four hundred square yards of concreted
surface, occupied by buildings made with cement and steel girders—now
seemed a kind of weird glacial desert—a desert set down on top of the living
soil, a tidy, planned desert, at once accommodating and abrasive, and self-
contained, that is, equipped with an absolute, all-inclusive scheme of
things, in which movement of bicycle + wilderness of streets echoing women's footsteps + trickle of water seeping along a crack in the macadam +
railings in sharp perspective + an almost complete absence of loud, shatter-
ing noises + fourteen storeys + cold air in frozen blocks like slabs of marble
and a flurry of artificial rain smelling of polythene indicated the exact steps
that had to be taken, plotted the rules of the inhuman game. (1–2; G 9–10)

Now he is trapped within it—the only end of the game being "this
very spot, the opposite of the site of the treasure, whose pirate and
crocodile lie in wait together" (2; G 10). Gone is Peter Pan, man's
immortality, imminent is inevitable death, the end of the world, the
Apocalypse.

LeClézio tries to make us aware of this in *The Flood* just as the
blind man teaches Besson to hear the flood. In fact the Four Horsemen ride through the novel. War is depicted in the opening pages
and is a game that Besson plays when alone in his room; it therefore
has a central place in the story also. Plague is there in the form of the
dying dog and the treatise on rabies. Famine is represented by
Besson's own hunger, which produces a trancelike state, during
which François imagines falling into a loaf of newly baked bread; and
the image of famine is present in the scene in the soup kitchen.
Death is everywhere. The references to death and destruction, the
images encompassing decomposition, are legion. The opening and
closing sections of the book, lyric and menacing, full of images and
prophesy, resemble in their very style the vision of St. John.

The world through which these horrors ride is seething with men
and man-made objects, with noise and hostility right to its very
molecular structure. The world is movement of matter. The descriptions of the city remind us constantly of this and of the contrast
between living matter and dead matter, motion and immobility, the
heat of energy and the cold of its loss. The city is an abomination

from which man cannot escape unless he is prepared to exile himself from his kind. (Besson never leaves its bounds on any of his walks.)

Man is trapped in a labyrinth of his own construction while playing, with all his strength and concentration, for the highest stakes, like the child at the pinball machine. But by studying himself, the human body, he realizes that what he is really doing is playing a role in a dance of death.[2]

The Flood is a siren of warning and alarm in the face of an appraisal of the human situation. Man is in the heart of a storm; a flood is preparing itself beneath his feet and all he can do is refuse to see. There is no Noah preparing for this deluge. Mankind is doomed.

V   *The Artist's Dance of Death: personal consciousness*

The Flood contains a more personal cry of despair also, wrung this time from the throat of the artist and expressed mainly in Anna Passeron's first tape. Clearly, writing was the activity which enabled Anna to cope with the world around her. The letters she exchanged with François in the past were an undeniable contact with someone else. But she lost faith, first in her reader: "Even if I could be certain you'd understand" (53; G 55); then in herself and her intentions: "Pure dumb egotism. Plus the urge to expose yourself, let other people gobble you up" (54; G 55); and finally in the value of the writing itself: "It serves no purpose, there isn't any truth in it. I mean, you don't make any discoveries or isolate any area of knowledge, you just wallow in illusion" (54; G 55). The whole sequence is an appeal for reassurance, reassurance of the need for art and the good faith of readers. Reassurance that this is not a mere game for others, because it touches the writer too deeply for him to live with such an idea: "It's not so much what they actually say to you at the time—what I can't stand, what really disgusts me, is the thought that when you've left they'll still be at it with some other victim. *They* couldn't care less" (55; G 56). The story of Albert is Anna's autobiography, an allegory of François' situation, and, one is very tempted to add, of LeClézio's also. If the snail cannot communicate he will die. Clearly, Anna cannot communicate or Paul would not have been able to leave her after reading the story. François is in the same situation or Anna would have replied to his letter more quickly—yet he does not reply to her tape. Each is shut off from the other and nonetheless must attempt to communicate. After his war game François writes also, but he is reduced to making lists of separate words and writing an affirmation of his action: "I am writing that I am writing that I am writing that I am writing" (130; G 126). The sentence is in fact an accurate statement of the situation. LeClézio is writing that François is writing down the fact that he is in the process of writing. Later François will destroy all his papers. Anna will destroy herself.

LeClézio's position is a strange one, if he has indeed lost faith in literature at this time, because being very much in Anna's shoes, he must write to stay alive—yet writing down one's lack of faith in what one is doing is hardly a healthy pursuit. He recognises this in an interview with Pierre Kyria at the time *The Flood* was published: "I write because I have a certain lack of equilibrium and writing is an equilibrium. But it's a dangerous equilibrium because the more one searches the more one destroys oneself."[3] Thus the novel is not only an appeal to help mankind but also reveals a very conscious expression of anguish on the part of the writer.

VI   *The Individual's Dance of Death: archetypal scream*

Under both of the above levels of desperation lies a third which embraces many of us in its struggle. François Besson is afraid to be alive. This fear expresses itself in a dislike of being looked at, an impression of being surrounded by eyes, and an acute sensitivity to the presence of woman, to whom his attitude is ambivalent. He is particularly aware of women old enough to be his mother and, indeed, when questioned about his mother he replies: "I love her to distraction, I loathe her guts, I despise her, I believe in her. She's—well, she's my mother, don't you understand?" (152; G 146).

His behavior toward younger women is one of indifference, but his hostility to all woman bursts out after he has left home for the last time: "On the big hoarding [billboard], where the posters were wrinkling now from a mixture of paste and rain, was a line of red-cheeked women, displaying cruel-looking rows of teeth, smiling with pale and cannibal mouths, while their dark eyes, capped by moustache-like sets of eyelashes, resembled so many giant heavy-legged spiders" (206; G 195).

Why should women become the enemy at this time? Because we are dealing with a reenactment of the trauma of birth. Whether LeClézio really intended us to take seriously the opening sentences of the preface to *Fever* or not; his statement, "If you really want to know, I should have preferred never to have been born," is borne out by the underlying theme of *The Flood*. In *Fever* he continues, "Of course, now it's done and I can't change it. But deep inside me there will always be this regret which spoils everything." The regret would seem to be operating here. Besson retires frequently to his room and shuts himself in, remaining immobile for long periods. He likes to be in the dark, likes to be in the rain, and during the storm crawls out to where the salt water will flow around and over him. He admires the blind man's position in the doorway, which resembles that of a fetus. Given all these details, Besson's final emergence from his room in a trail of fire is evidently a symbolic depiction of birth. Soon afterward he is alone and hungry; his hostility toward women then, at this point, is that of a baby expelled from the comfort of the womb into a cold outside world. Besson's confession then becomes his baptism when he is cleansed of original sin.

The most explicit expression of his resentment comes however when he is sitting outside at night, cold and afraid. He kills the unknown man and walks up the tunnel to the sea—in other words, he refuses to take on the figure of a man and reverses the birth process totally: "He plunged forward through the closed cylinder where no daylight ever penetrated, his whole body exposed and in agony, like a small scrap of reason and common sense afloat on the bitter ocean of folly" (241; G 228). To believe in his own reinsertion into the womb it is essential that he should not see—and, being blind, he is put back into the surrogate womb in which we first found him—his room. LeClézio may not be able to reverse his own birth, but Besson managed to do so instead.

VII *Myth*

François retreats from his new vision of the world by blinding himself because he cannot bear the reality it reveals. Anna kills herself. From this culmination we can see a first link between *The Flood* and the story of Oedipus. Other links are scattered throughout the novel.

Oedipus left home because he was afraid he would kill his father and marry his mother, as had been prophesied by the oracle of Apollo. He killed an unknown man and answered the questions asked by the sphinx that was ravaging the city—then killed the sphinx and married the queen Jocasta. Many years later the city was plague-ridden and to cure it the murderer of Laius the king had to be found. It was Oedipus. As a result of the revelation Jocasta killed herself and Oedipus put out his eyes (as described in Sophocles' *Oedipus the King*). The blind man wanders around Greece and as an old man finally seems to be at one with the universe (*Oedipus at Colonnus*).

From the first part of the legend Freud took the components of his Oedipus complex—the desire of any little boy to replace his father in his mother's life.

In *The Flood* both Greek and psychoanalytical elements are mixed. To begin with François Besson's way of blinding himself, it is clear that he is sacrificing himself to the sun—two clear indications have been given already: Marthe tells him his favorite color is sun color, and Besson himself describes the power of the sun: "Eyes wide open, Besson gazed at the area dominated by the sun, it was like an abyss, a silent maelstrom sunk into the heavens. Everything, absolutely everything moved centripetally towards it: even the mind, with its caravans of thoughts and ideas, was irresistibly attracted by this dazzling focal point. To struggle against it was out of the question: you had no time to put up any defence, before you knew what had happened you were its slave" (159; G 153). The sun is Apollo, hence, like Oedipus, François is in the power of the sun and meets the fate he described in oracular form at the beginning of the novel: "Like a loudspeaker in reverse, the window's gullet swallowed up the sum of all noises in the town, and left nothing but a *tragic* calm behind. No one could *look steadily at it* without flinching: it was a second sun, black and mournful, spreading out its rays of darkness" (8; G 15). Here are the room, tragedy, blindness, and sun linked for us before we can understand their meaning. Besson, like Oedipus, takes on the misery of the city, and only when he has sacrificed himself in horror does he begin to understand the world and its mysteries:

Behind the rampart of mist and ruin, I know, paradise lies concealed. But this paradise is one that needs must remain lost to us, since no road to its attainment exists. Such are harmony and beauty. Everything was swift, logical, well-defined. This was the time of that mystery that I bore within myself all unawares, and which bound all things together one with another. It was neither faith nor passion, but a delicate subtle joy, the perfect virtue of a shadow hermetically sealed in a box, cohesion in thought and deed, a reunited family about to sit down to table. And all this was irremediably destroyed by the acuteness of a pair of eyes, the agony of two retinas, the exacerbated functioning of nerves and cells. (282; G 266)

He continues later: "The eye must penetrate to the very heart of matter, cutting a path with agony and fever and palpitations of the heart—through millions of molecules. Deeper still then, at the core of cloud and vapor, the eye must become number, must pierce further, while molecules separate and matter divides, till it reaches the uncharitable point of mathematical bewilderment, that point X of anguish and despair where all physical matter ends and nothing remains beyond it but the empty void" (290; G 274); and finally, with a quotation from a seventeenth century meditation on death the circle is closed. François Besson shares the cosmic vision of Oedipus at Colonnus and has penetrated the depths of his original terror produced when he began to see death everywhere. The opening section foretold his fate, the last closes it in glory: "Rising through light like the length of a drawn sword, passing joyfully into that agonising effulgence, he vanishes from sight as the boiling, turbulent mass closes over him; moves on with it now, up, up, to the topmost peaks of the world, plunged naked into the volcano's maw, carried up to that field of black azure that lies beyond all human values. Made light. Purified" (300; G 283).

This death he sees is the parallel to the state of Thebes under Oedipus and, like Oedipus, during the search for the cause of such a state of affairs, he relives parts of his life. The elements are the same as those of Oedipus but as we are rather in analysis than legend with Besson, the story does not emerge in one piece. We see François first with his mother and later with Marthe. We can assume that the situation of Marthe and Lucas is the ideal one—the boy has no father to oppose him. Lucas is not happy to meet François and his games and dreams are those of violence and death—of ogres, vampires, werewolves trying to kill the child who is immortal. Lucas is afraid of the danger a father represents. This episode would seem to be that of the Oedipus complex reenacted before François' eyes, in which case François' nights with Marthe are those of Oedipus with Jocasta. Certainly they were preceded by numerous questions. Marthe is both sphinx and mother combined.

Like the young Oedipus, François leaves home; like him also François goes to the temple and consults the oracle to find out whether he is in the favor of the gods. Like Oedipus he is given an enigmatic answer. He kills an unknown man and leaves his homeland, to become the victim of Apollo as had been ordained.

The myth, with all its complex implications, is there, beneath the surface of the text, transforming the despair into an archetypal situation encompassing the whole world and into a neurosis; thus the cosmic and the personal are again joined, to increase the impact of both.

VIII *Narration*

All of the levels of interpretation discussed clarify to some extent the problem posed by the mode of narration of the novel. The main part of the story is told about François Besson and refers to him in the third person; but in the opening section we encounter changes from *Je, François Besson* (21) to the second person familiar form *tu* and then *il*, while the closing section goes from first person to second person formal *vous* and third person. These shifts would seem to indicate Besson's variable attitudes to himself: acceptance (*je*), friendliness (*tu*), total separation (*il*) and recognition but distancing (*vous*) and also the various stages of relationship between LeClézio himself and the story he is telling.

Primarily these changes occur in the opening and closing sections of the book in which we are perceiving and contemplating the outside world with Besson. We are inside his anguish and experience it with him. Hence the changes throw light on his state of mind.

IX *Conclusion*

François Besson is an excessive character with a multitude of social problems. He is the portrait of a neurotic with the bearing of a prophet. Is he mad or is our world in the state he describes? By making madness a possibility LeClézio is again begging the question and, as in *The Interrogation*, is offering us a way of rejecting what he has to say. This is, however, not an easy thing to do.

The Flood transmits to us an anguish and an awareness which it is difficult to ignore; through the detailed description of Besson's actions, the people and places that surround him, we live his increasing alienation, his approaching moment of deliberate destruction. It is a powerful metaphor of the *malaise* of our time and has a force that is not born of the imagination alone.

CHAPTER 5

The Ecstasy of Matter

The Ecstasy of Matter is a new phase in LeClézio's writing; he has left the realm of fiction in order to express his personal philosophy in the form of an essay. The book consists of a series of discursive meditations on various questions that have manifested themselves already in his novels and short stories. And this is perhaps its major interest, for it throws light on recurrent symbols and images by showing what each means to the author. The book gains in clarity as it advances; while some of the later sections are a pleasure to read the beginning is rather chaotic. This is partly because in the beginning LeClézio is expressing his original confusion and problems; yet the cosmic writing we have already encountered in the opening chapter of *The Flood* is not easy to follow. (The easiest way to get into the book is to allow the lyrico-philosophical language to flow over one the first time without making any attempt to understand it and to come back and read it again at the end.) Unfortunately, the form of the essay frees the weaker elements of the author's style from the constraints imposed by characterization and plot; parts of *The Ecstasy of Matter* are therefore verbose and the final section is very repetitive. These disadvantages aside, the book is an interesting one and certainly merits our attention. It would be useful to work through the ideas at some length.

I *Form*

The essay takes a similar form to that of *The Flood:* it has an opening section entitled *The Ecstasy of Matter;* a long central section, *The Infinitely Average,* which is divided into nine chapters, eight of which have titles of their own; and a final section called *Silence,* which brings many of the arguments formulated early in the book to their conclusion in some kind of death. The first section treats the world and its movements at the level of circulation of matter before the birth of the author, and the central part deals with the author's position during his life. Hence we have a cycle from void to void. In LeClézio's words: ". . . between the infinitely huge and the infinitely tiny there is the infinitely average" (G 106). The infinitely average, as we shall see, is the matter that makes up a human existence.

II   "The Ecstasy of Matter"

Before the author's birth he existed through others as particles in them. At his birth these particles would be united for a certain length of time to create him and then would be separated again. Each individual life lasts only an instant. The world lasts and exists for itself: "The world was on this side, enveloping, real, and elusive solidarity which has no resolution, matter which it is impossible to feel, impossible to love or understand, matter full and long whose justification was neither external nor internal but itself" (G 10). Everything has an identity and importance within the pattern and rhythm of the whole. There is nothing to understand. The world is in a state of creation, mysterious, gratuitous, and continuous. The whole is dominated by the sun, its light and heat, and by the night which brings an awareness of the void. This void, this darkness, is the essential opposition to the threat of the sun and is vital to LeClézio's concept of his own situation. Here he writes: "This is the only place; in it everything is encompassed. This black and sacred gulf is the only reality. It cannot be denied. Whatever one does one can only come forth from it, live in it, and return to it, one does not leave it" (G 21); and as no understanding is possible, one should open oneself to the void in order to feel all the particles of matter in their places in the universe "and not want to hope for anything except that which the world offered by the simple fact of being there" (G 22).

This is the journey that we shall undertake in various ways throughout the book and which we return to at the very end.

III   "The Infinitely Average"

Language creates a reality which is in fact an illusion and which ties man into society, not even allowing him the freedom to be himself. This assertion leads to a discussion of the state of existence and the effect others have on one's life—the fact that one cannot choose one's own end. "Nothing comes from us, nothing belongs to us. We are only ways through" (G 28)—as screens on which the past throws a dim light which we in turn throw into the future. (Light is necessary to life.) Hence the only thing we can do is live the present totally. The next paragraphs explore aspects of this life.

Culture is a social game. It can and should be one kind of food that man provides, but art is not reality.

Next comes consciousness of the body. We should pay it more attention, for it fights to keep us alive every moment of our lives: "Being alive is perpetual uncertainty. And the swinging movement continues between fullness and emptiness, between that which belongs to me and that which is negation of all property" (G 35). This contrast is the essence of life: "Life and nothingness, emptiness and fullness balance each other continually, are one within the other, indistinguishably mingled. To live is to be dead and death is active. Just as the infinite is made of finiteness and the finite is the birth of the infinite, these apparent contradictions resolve themselves in a realm beyond words. . . . We are written there as the rock and our will has no effect" (G 35). Or rather, it is life; for to quote LeClézio once more: "One of the mistakes in analysis is to make a distinction between form and content. It is quite clear that form and content are one and the same and that it is absolutely impossible to separate them" (G 36). One is what one is—the idea is the words in which it is expressed—language is made of the same stuff as reality: "It is the indissoluble unity of the comprehensible world, language" (G 37). The importance here lies in the word *comprehensible.* Words can separate matter into objects, actions, etc., but as we have seen above, they are unable to grasp the real world in which everything comes together.

There is therefore a basic problem which LeClézio is struggling with here and throughout the essay concerning reality (which is unknowable) and the comprehensible (and communicable) world. He will try and solve the problem by contemplating reality (but what is he contemplating?), accepting his position of nonchoice consciously and using it to work toward lucidness.

The contemplation will take two aspects: "As for me, my heart goes toward form and my reason toward diversity" (G 41).

The cause of man's suffering is that he can neither give himself over to form without being caught in the jungle of life nor let himself be absorbed by the multitudinousness without regretting the systematic ways of thought he has abandoned. But these diverse perceptions, if ever they could come together, would perhaps build by their very dialectic, the revelation, the understanding the author is seeking.

The rest of the central section is made up of meditations, reflections, observations of existence (in so far as it is within the grasp of LeClézio), which turn around these poles of structure, multitudinous detail, and suffering. Within the scope of this book it is not possible to analyse such diversity and, indeed, its value comes largely from personal meditation of the reader on the thoughts offered by the author. He takes us through his relation to the physical world, various ways of understanding his personal situation (including writing and art), and into the realm of doubt, darkness, and death.

Death has two forms: the physical kind and the kind that comes from mirrors, dark windows, and open books—which are reflections of reality, both dangerous and symbolic. Man sees reflections of himself this way; and in seeing death in life opposes his self to the void of his imagined death in order to find comfort. Through the medium of sight he participates in life, tries to analyse and create systems. From what he sees and feels he creates all abstractions—emotions, gods, concepts—for there are no absolutes in the material world.

Man seeks refuge in society but must not simply abandon himself into the mass and lose his identity; for man has no other destiny than to be man. In what he calls despair, which arises from his noncomprehension of the gratuitousness of the world, lies his liberty: "Whoever has been able to accept himself as a tragic figure, who has been able to be the hero of his life, may perhaps understand the world. He has made himself man, and society can be born in him. He has refused no reality however despairing, for everything that came to him, he felt as if it were part of himself. Ideas are alive: everything in the mind must be concordant with matter. The world is not shaped according to the demands of thought; the domain of the lived determines the way language and ideas are expressed" (G 182). At this point a man who has thoroughly explored his own narrow place on earth can escape perhaps beyond himself into the universal.

IV   "*Silence*"

This is what man can achieve during his lifetime. The final section deals, then, with death. There is a certain iteration of points made in the opening chapter of the essay, with the idea that man is not made to last and, at death, will be reintegrated into the matter of the universe. This inevitably carries its reciprocal, that he who is reintegrated is dead. Words, objects, writing, everything leads to death, because they lead to the greatest idea man ever has: that it is possible not to be a man. And as no system can be founded on man, the individual must rid himself of others who turn back reflections of himself and of themselves also for each is the image of the other. Thus they reflect back and forth to infinity and hence to nothingness. (This is an idea treated early in "The Infinitely Average.") But, in fact, as death is in life, sometimes manifesting itself in the garb of life, and all aspects of life and death are inseparable, everything is working toward the void whether man wishes or no.

Two deaths, two voids—one in the spaces of the universe, the other inside man, where consciousness can turn in on itself and think of itself thinking, tossing self-consciousness back and forth, into the self, where it becomes the darkness of infinity, like reflections in parallel mirrors, "the infinitely human." Death gives the extra sense by which one is aware, by which one can know: "Thanks to him, I was again linked to chaos and I did not lose sight of the void" (G 221). The "dead man" in the self is, therefore, the part of a man which is in the closest contact with the matter from which he came and to which he will return. It is the "dead man" that gives awareness and that enables man to create for himself some kind of peace and harmony with the field in which he is a figure, that helps him to go beyond the distinctions, created by language and society in the interest of communication and cohesion, into the realm of undifferentiated matter.

V   The Ecstasy of Matter *and Zen*

LeClézio's position in the essay is reminiscent of descriptions of students of Zen who are given some insoluble problem by their master and beat their brains upon it, until finally they realize that it is insoluble because there is no problem except one they are creating for themselves by believing that a problem exists. LeClézio's book follows this example by beginning in a confusing way and becoming clearer and clearer in its statements.

There is, however, more to the similarity than that. Zen is a way of liberation, a way of changing a person's conception of the world around him in such a way that he no longer creates false problems for himself and so can achieve serenity. This serenity would seem to come from four major sources: removal of social pressure, an ability to live within one's means in the present, the dissociation of the individual from an awareness based in selfhood, and an acceptance of the universe as an undivided field. All of these sources are of some concern to LeClézio, as we have seen from the very beginning of *The Ecstasy of Matter*.

Any society puts a certain pressure on its citizens to behave in certain fashions in order to communicate certain comprehensible signs, to participate in its functions. To withdraw from such pressure is something that we have seen a number of LeClézio's characters trying to do—notably Adam Pollo—and the only way they have been able to succeed is in denying the control they have over their withdrawal, that is, by going mad (losing their mind), hence renouncing all responsibility. In Zen a liberated man is a "no-mind,"[1] and this would seem to be the state toward which LeClézio is working. He struggles with the problem himself: "Another certainty: that of living irremediably in society, without being able to withdraw from it. . . . How can I be myself, how can I not communicate? I am involved body and soul in this society" (G 46). He continues his reasoning thus: "Those who believe they are detached are the same people who imagine that action is one thing, thought another. To think is to act, and to be oneself is to be other people. . . . The singular closes around the universal, and the universal always turns back to the singular. They [men] are only the minutest particle, the exact picture of everything they form and which encompasses them. Whoever wants to be one is several and it is by being several that he is one" (G 46–47). With this he moves out beyond the conception of an individual in society into an awareness in which the notion of self as a separate entity has disappeared, to be replaced by one where subject and object are no longer divided and where the human is not apart from the rest.

He has reached a Zen attitude which implies nondivision in a universe which cannot be analysed by man:

For man everything ends in contradiction, mystery, because everything is cohesion. The world is indissociable. It forms a single unit. If it has reasons, if it has a finality, if it has an origin, they are all mixed together with present time; they are an integral part of what we think of as products, postulates, and consequences. Cause and effect are one and the same. The pure phenomenon contains its evolution and its static state at the same time, and both its individual peculiarity and its dependence. (G 170)

Thus things which are usually considered as separate come together in a *yin-yang* relationship which recurs throughout the essay, especially with reference to life and death: "Life and death are unimportant categories like vegetable or mineral. Life and death are forms that matter adopts among many others" (*G* 161). The world is indivisible; and as Lao-tzu wrote, "When everyone recognizes goodness to be good, there is already evil. Thus to be and not to be arise mutually."[2] (We have seen elsewhere the interdependency of light and darkness, rain and sun, throughout LeClézio's work.)

The problem of comprehending the world in this way lies in the communication of the understanding. We need to be able to express knowledge in words—a problem for all LeClézio's protagonists—and language cannot always cope with such demands. LeClézio writes: "Each time I turn toward joy, horror appears. And the two always mingle, arise together, resonate in me as one and the same emotion. Shiver from pleasure and shiver from fear. Feel enjoyment or pain. There is no possible system, no language which expresses the truth. It is too confused, too mixed up. There is no word for these two states which are in fact one" (*G* 86). Such a perception must needs be unspoken and tends therefore to a mystical consciousness of the nondivision of the world. This is a state LeClézio and his protagonists are feeling their way toward, and it is one which the masters of Zen seek to create continually in their students; for from this state it is a short step to liberation. Liberation is seeing the world in a new way: "While Rikko, a high government official of the T'ang dynasty, had a talk with his Zen master Nansen, the official quoted a saying of Sojo, a noted monk-scholar of an earlier dynasty: 'Heaven and earth and I are of the same root/ The ten-thousand things and I are of one substance,' and continued, 'Is not this a remarkable statement?' " Nansen called the attention of the visitor to the flowering plant in the garden and said, "People of the world look at these flowers as if they were in a dream."[3]

Here the subject-object split has disappeared. There is no alienation between man and his world, and the problems of Adam Pollo, François Besson, and the others cannot occur. Adam had perhaps the best attitude to the world in his game-playing (though he was doing it as the fool rather than the sage); for from a true observance of the world comes the idea that it is all a game, in the sense that since everything is inseparable and gratuitous no choice is important. Le Clézio writes, "The matter from which I am made dances its ballet for no reason" (*G* 179). Seng-ts'an replies:

> The perfect Way is without difficulty,
> Save that it avoids picking and choosing. . . .
> If you want to get the plain truth,
> Be not concerned with right and wrong.
> The conflict between right and wrong
> Is the sickness of the mind.[4]

At the end of *The Ecstasy of Matter* Le Clézio has a vision of an undivided universe in which nature *is* the pattern (rather than conforming to a pattern) and man is part of matter (rather than being an alien individual). LeClézio realizes that man must study himself, must know himself to know others. The mind reflecting itself has produced what he calls "the dead man" in himself which has opened up a third eye: "This gaze carried me beyond my senses, beyond my illusions; it was the real in me, the me in me. It set to work on my knowledge, a sun in that night, and made me *know*. Thanks to it, I was joined to chaos and never lost sight of the void" (*G* 221). Whether his aim is that of Zen, as "the infinitely average" would lead us to believe, or not, it would seem very similar in its aspirations. When we remember that LeClézio spent 1966 in Bangkok and that he quoted Eastern texts already in this master's thesis,[5] the idea is not as strange as it may have appeared at first; and his last words certainly lead us to believe that he is on a quest, be it for death in either of the forms he describes, or understanding: ". . . without understanding it, but being sure that I was doing it, I began the long religious journey which, no doubt, will never end" (*G* 222)—a journey which will take him into the heart of matter as a collection of its particles, where he will finally achieve *The Ecstasy of Matter*.

VI   The Ecstasy of Matter *and the Previous Fiction*

The passage which has the most bearing on LeClézio's work is a subsection of "The Trap," and in order to look at it in detail it will be useful to quote it at length:

Night and death. The relationships are known and they are not imaginary. *Man needs to see. He lives only because he sees, because he knows.* The gaze, the gaze which judges and gives consciousness is also the means of survival, the best shield and the surest dagger. Before struggling, before undertaking anything, he looks and he judges. And in his eyes there passes a little of the awful intelligence which can reduce things. Then, when this gaze encounters nothing more, the intelligence slides along on those rails which are lost in the infinite veils of the unknowable, then fear, anguish, and doubt are born, then begins the reign of demons. Terrible night where nothing is touched, night which suddenly instates the void in the world which was previously so full and hard, night which comes to haunt and which perhaps recalls, deep inside us, a very distant, very vague memory of the nothingness we have known. *Night of the intelligence which, having become blind, turns in on itself, and where the nightmare begins before sleep.* Do the gods come from here? Is this the cause of this anguish, this doubt, this *malaise* in us? Like the rhythm of tides and sun flares, *the rhythm of day and night casts a spell on our thoughts.* It shapes them, and if we no longer recognize them as coming directly from the forces of nature, at least we feel what perceptible, memorable anguish there is spread out around us which binds us, holds us, tortures us [*sic*]. . . .

Perhaps there are two forces which pull us toward the great beyond; two violent and contradictory forces whose confrontation we have copied in our minds: fear born of night, a reminder of death, the force of sleep, of evil, of hell. But also *the anguish of bright daylight, the terrible sense of being crushed in the face of the hardness and inaccessibility of the sun.* While one pulls us downward, makes us see monsters and crime, the other catches hold of us and hauls us toward the virgin summits, *makes us breathe the extent of being, the unique, the revealed, ecstasy itself.*

But neither of these two forces is really favorable to man. Night and day, emptiness and fullness, thus conceived, are two monsters eager to inflict suffering and destruction.

Daytime anguish is perhaps even more terrifying than that of the night. For here we are not prey to a vicious enemy who always slips away: we are faced with the hardness, cruelty and pitiless violence of the real. Ours is not a fear of an unknown, digging its pit but of an exasperation of the being, a sort of dizziness caused by existence which as it spreads and shows itself exterminates us. *That which is too visible is even more hostile than the invisible. It burns, it is relentless, it dislocates man's soul and separates his mind from matter.* It makes life look larger than life. *It creates the mad hope of an absolute universe, beyond man, a universe magnificently and eternally full and visible, and utterly inaccessible.* In the face of this the conscious no longer encounters permeable objects, or intelligible signs but the immense plan of a frozen enigma where harmony is beyond reach. Monotheism, born of the cults of the sun, demands that the living should be crushed. The spectacle which is shown to us with such intensity, with such incandescence, is a spectacle of the supraintelligible. Under the single ferocious eye staring at the earth is the reign of vengeance, destiny, and damnation.

Sole God of day, and millions of gods of night, you have shared the world between you; and between your alternating reigns, *man's spirit*, by turns crushed and lost, given up to odious and brutal impermeability or to aimless communication with the unknown, *has become detached from matter and has lost harmony* (had he, in fact, ever known it?). Alien forces, forces, forces, which are in nature, forces which are in the mind, enemies, enemies, I hate you. I bow down, I adore you. But I hate you. I hate you.

Between these two abysses, the one rising up, the other hollowed out, where can I find comfort? Where can I find the space which will allow me to rest, love, and perhaps understand? Where can I find a little solitude? Where? Oh! Where? (*G* 136–38; all italics are mine)

First we see the impact this passage has on our understanding of François Besson in *The Flood*. His self-inflicted blindness shows, as we have already said, a refusal of the world, a refusal to try and understand what is going on around him, hence a refusal of life-death. François Besson has killed himself just as Anna has. This death can be one of two kinds however: physical death or mental death. Mental death occurs when the mind turns in on itself and becomes conscious of nothing but the very fact that it is conscious. It reflects itself back and forth into infinity—the infinite void. LeClézio explains the progression in "Conscience" (*G* 152–54): "The most terrible action of the mind is perhaps this closure: when, abandoning all precise aim, the internal gaze is wholly occupied in that one exploit which is to be conscious of its own consciousness. . . . Tragic grandeur of thought which perhaps has its culmination in that perfection which is also its death. . . . The absolute of thought is to think thought. Strange limit and strange absolute since it is a reflection. The ultimate wall limiting consciousness is a mirror which directs inward." So François Besson has turned in on himself to such an extent that he is living in a nightmare of sensitivity and self-awareness. At this point "the gaze which judges and gives consciousness [and] is also the means of survival; the best shield" becomes "the surest dagger." Other people's gaze is dangerous. It is to escape his awareness of other people's judgment of himself that he refuses to see, as much as it is his refusal to understand other people.

Besson is a man of the night who worries, fears, suffers anguish, as Beaumont does, and yet it is the sun which destroys his sight. This emergence into the light is an indication that his anguish has developed until he is unable to avoid the hostility of the world around him any longer and his position, lying on the beach, shows him literally crushed by his fear and by the inaccessibility of the sun. It is in trying to penetrate this inaccessibility that he sinks into the void. He is destroyed by the forces of might and day.

The above passage has equal importance for our understanding of *The Interrogation*. Adam Pollo is influenced by light and heat. His is the opposite temperament from that of Besson; nonetheless he is ultimately destroyed. He is searching to understand the matter which surrounds him—he tries to become a pebble, lichen, a dog—but is utterly unable to do so because, we are told here, the sun dislocates man's soul and separates his spirit from matter. Adam's passion for systems, his desire to be within a coherent one, is explained also by LeClézio's association of the sun with the desire for an absolute universe which is totally beyond man's reach. Such a universe leads LeClézio to monotheism: "Monotheism, born of solar cults, demands that living things should be crushed" and we see why Adam should be linked with Apollo and why he should be defeated: The Fall gains a new perspective as a necessity in an absolute structure. At the same time the slaughter of the rat is included in the final sentence of the paragraph: "Under the unique and ferocious eye which stares at the earth is the reign of vengeance, destiny and damnation." Such a system is one which stresses the power and uniqueness of the godhead, which is constructed on the unique source of strength and therefore breeds mysticism, identification with the god and the ecstasy thus produced. Adam's final speech is the culmination of such a development, the rat scene being an earlier stage.

In the light of the quotation from "The Trap" it becomes important to take into account the time of day at which each story in *Fever* takes place also; for each "fever" will draw its characteristics from the part of the daily cycle at which it occurs. Roche Estève's derangement is not of the nature of Beaumont's. Beaumont is prey to a thousand fears, whereas Estève becomes violent, aggressive—his character changes until he finally loses himself altogether into the body of a woman. Beaumont never escapes from himself; rather, it is the objects around him that manifest hostility.

In every case, however, we have the description of "the spirit of man by turns crushed and lost, given up to odious and brutal impermeability or to aimless communication with the unknown which is detached from matter and has lost its harmony." *The Ecstasy of*

Matter provides a summary and an interpretation of all the previous work, and the end of the passage quoted connects the writing intimately with the state of mind of LeClézio himself.

VII *Conclusion*

The Ecstasy of Matter is perhaps an easier book to read and understand than it is to analyse. Following in many ways the precepts it contains, it provides a dialectic between man's desire to organize his world and the seething masses of material with which he has to deal. The unifying thread is the personal quest of the author for some kind of understanding. In pursuing his thought, he elaborates a view of the world which not only helps the reader understand Le Clézio's earlier work but which is extremely interesting in its own right.

CHAPTER 6

Terra Amata

Terra Amata relates to *The Ecstasy of Matter* in the same way that Camus' literary work related to his essays. *The Ecstasy of Matter* offers a philosophy of life, in the sense of giving a description of what it is like to be alive, a living particle in a material universe. *Terra Amata* is a description of a life in which the vast panorama of swirling detail has been curtailed and translated into the actions and attitudes making up the existence of the fictional character Chancelade. The meditations have been rendered concrete. *The Ecstasy of Matter* was the search for a theory behind life. *Terra Amata* is the practice.

I *Résumé*

Chancelade as a small child imprisons and kills insects. When he gets a bit older he prefers to go to the beach rather than to school. He draws. His father dies and we see the funeral procession. Then Chancelade is older. He spends three days in a hotel with Mina. Later he marries her—one hot day he leaps out of the car into the crowd. Another day he is on the beach with his son. Throughout are discussions of life, death, truth, lies, and communication of various kinds. Chancelade feels himself to be in a world which sends back reflections all the time. Driven into a fever by this feeling he goes to the top of a high-rise building and talks to God. After this he is more aware of death and the approaching void. Finally we see him as an old man. He goes for a walk and warns a young girl of the brevity of life. He dies.

The best résumé would be the poem created by listing the titles of the chapters,

> On the earth by chance
> I was born

a living man
I grew up
inside the drawing
the days went by
and the nights
I played all those games
loved
happy
I spoke all those languages
gesticulating
saying incomprehensible words
or asking indiscreet questions
in a region that resembled hell
I peopled the earth
to conquer the silence
to tell the whole truth
I lived in the immensity of consciousness
I ran away
then I grew old
I died
and was buried

(209; G 234)

II *Chancelade*

Chancelade has many characteristics in common with other
LeClézio heroes and, indeed, with LeClézio himself. Tall, blond,
blue-eyed, he has a wife called Mina, which could well be a diminu-
tive of Marina, the name of LeClézio's wife.

Like the author and his creations he is, from time to time, a
walking man and his walking is a sign of his unease in the world, his
alienation from the people around him. He is alone in the crowd but
less pathologically so than Adam Pollo, Paoli, Besson, and the
others, and we see him there less frequently. Chancelade is not
constantly pursued by the hostile gaze of the outside world and will
become neither mad nor blind. Indeed, the first time we see him in
a crowd is at the fair, and he is accompanied by Mina.

III *Chancelade and Women*

Chancelade's dealings with women are much happier than those
of his predecessors. He plays with the little girl and accepts her
advances quite patiently as a boy. Later, with Mina, he experiences
a violent happiness, an awareness of being alive, and an appreciation

of it that has never previously occurred in LeClézio's writing. He has achieved a semblance of contact with another human being and writes: "How were you to say you were happy, at that moment, on that part of the earth, with that woman, with yourself, and with everything else? It wasn't easy to say, and yet you had to say it. You had to forget the fatal issue, pain, decay, the minute but effective assaults of time. You had to forget the void, the being abandoned, the being alone and live out your own adventure with joy. Nothing counted anymore but this explosion of life, an explosion beautiful and unique" (85, G 98).

Admittedly his attempt to declare his love to Mina in Morse code with an electric torch proves fruitless, but, in the café, they are able to communicate between themselves (in deaf and dumb language) while the rest of the world is excluded. It is not until later, after we have seen him with a twelve-year old son, that he describes sexual contact as something to occupy the time when nothing else is left.

The danger of women, clearly manifested in *The Interrogation* and *The Flood,* has been mitigated, though the sensation of being absorbed back into the eternal woman remains—intercourse is a return to the womb and through it an infusion into the whole body of woman. Roche Estève experienced it first during his fever and Chancelade shares his experience: "For a few seconds everything in the world was woman. . . . /For a moment Chancelade managed to struggle against the cool white tide that slowly rolled his body over and over; then he gave in and became a woman, the same invincible woman who possessed the earth from the dazzling center of her body, and who was no more either thought or word, but simply a sign of life eternally deployed throughout the universe" (144; G 163). The content of this quotation is essentially the same as that of a poem published for the first time in 1963[1], and quoted below. There is, however, a marked difference in the attitude of the author toward woman.

> You think you know you're suffering
> or that you're alone; all this is
> serious; and today, as a result
> of walking up and down
> worked hard like animals
> out of breath, you discover
> ferocious conquests.
> today, opposite woman

suddenly, space
lightening fury, in a minute
and then light, light (not)
daylight sickness, you no longer see
the naked woman.
She believes. You feel her
move confusedly
in the bosom of a childish terror
You remember that she
threw you barefooted into the world
suckled at her gigantic breast
sang, and very quietly,
warmly, in a woollen voice
against your ear, multiform
melodies, which people
heads like books.
And you see her naked, yes
on the pillow, struck
right in the belly of capable
desires, wanting you
to crush her, to buy her,
buy in handfuls.
She is still growing
becomes day, howls
in our pitiful ears
scarlet, hurls herself into the middle
of all memories
makes herself a monster of solitude
You sense she is suddenly so huge
so immaculate, yelling so, so
abusive, so hot with love and that,
So ferocious, above all so furious
that then
you are dumb
deaf, blind;
you hardly feel
with your very nerve-ends
an ever increasing chain;
afterwards, little by little,
day after day,
without paying anymore attention
to winds and mountains,
suns and snakes,
you know you are naked,

> you know she is naked,
> you know that together you are
> for ever,
> for a sort of eternity
> naked,
> naked,
> two earth animals
> since enlarged by furious desires,
> veritable continents of savages,
> or mountains of excrement, roots
> ecstasies, two black drawings
> that never a nerve will unite.

The text is here in full because it throws considerable light on Adam Pollo's behavior, and that of François Besson in particular, in contrast to the serenity achieved by Chancelade. Pollo and Besson are afraid of women, Chancelade is learning to accept them, although his view of them as all-engulfing has not changed. He accepts the feeling of being absorbed into womanhood as a temporary effect of ejaculation and detumescence and no longer fears total loss of identity. As a result his treatment of Mina has reached the stage of being a relationship rather than a hit and run sequence.

In the context of the poem the drawing in Chapter 6 is interesting also. The poem insists on an eternal separation between man and woman, two parallel solitudes, and we notice that although the boy and girl are holding hands, the background of the sketch refutes this testimony. It would seem evident that each pair of houses linked by a twisting path signifies one life from birth to death, and although the paths are similar and not far apart there is no link between them at any stage.

IV *Theme of Solitude*

It would seem that Chancelade is not as close to Mina as he believed, and he is aware of his distance from his son: "There was this child now that was not him, who lived a few inches from him, absolutely detached" (137; G 155). As an old man he remarks that everyone has been taken away from him; nevertheless, his deathbed is surrounded by figures who would seem to be the people he spoke about earlier: Mina, Emmanuelle, his friends. This solitude is the lot of man, and it shows itself in a number of ways. First we have the recurring image in LeClézio's work of the man in the crowd, the man walking alone (as we have mentioned previously). He is alone because the other people are not accessible to him. This is made quite clear in Chancelade's dream of the statues, where we have a psychological transposition of the effect of the crowd elsewhere in the novel:

> The statue sheds its masks furiously, like running water.
> And its face is never seen.
> It has no face, it has only millions of falling masks.
> Millions of fixed eyes.
> The statue will never show its real face.
> And in the same way, all along the walls of the great empty room, the millions of statues shed their masks, here their fixed eyes, there their hard noses, there again their empty mouths with two wrinkles on each side.
> The masks frantically come and go from one end to the other of the empty room.
> And not a single word is ever spoken   (57–58; G 69)

Then, in opposition to the nonattachment it represents, is offered the importance of names. *Terra Amata* is full of lists of animals, people, streets, occupations, because giving or knowing a name is a way of escaping solitude. LeClézio deals with the subject at some length early in the novel (5–10; G 12–17). He writes: "And when you'd given everything, each animal and each plant, a name, you'd never be alone again. All over this huge landscape . . . these names are linked with one another by fine, almost invisible threads" (7; G 14). Thus, when Chancelade gives a name to God he is trying desperately to pull Him into the adventures of every particle on earth: "Jacques Loubet, profession: infinite and eternal. . . . There, that means something. . . . I used to think it was daft just talking into thin air, just pretending to talk to someone. God—that doesn't mean anything. Nobody here's called that" (171; G 193). Knowing someone's name is the beginning of communication. It is striking how often Chancelade uses Mina's name in the chapters where they understand each other—for example, it appears nine times in the Morse message.

This can only have effect, of course, if the ways of communication are open and, in an ironic series of chapters, we are shown how frequently this is not so. LeClézio offers drawings, notes put into bottles or other unlikely places, messages carved on cactus leaves, word games of various sorts, animal and insect noises, Morse code, deaf and dumb, and various little known languages including Finnish and a gobbledygook of his own invention (I think!). To crack any of these message codes a great deal of effort has to be made, a great deal of chance is involved (that two people should understand the same one is amazing), and in some cases the attempt is hopeless. Thus it is when Chancelade talks to God.

Talking to God takes us out of the realm of noncommunication and into the vaster realm of the cosmic void. Throughout LeClézio's work we have encountered this concept of the void, which lies around everything in life and is its most powerful force. It is discussed at great length in *The Ecstasy of Matter* and the same ideas recur here.

Chancelade has his first sensation of emptiness at his father's funeral: "He had never seen so much emptiness, so much fated violence, so much fear and fatigue concentrated in such a small space. . . . Intelligence was suddenly overthrown, and you were swept by the current of tragedy through the icy regions of that which you do not understand, that which you never will understand, that of which you know you will always know nothing" (50; G* 60–61); and this feeling recurs from time to time, reaching its apogee immediately before his appeal to God. Chancelade is caught in a world where everything is reflecting back and forth in daylight and in darkness, producing the two kinds of void encountered in *The Ecstasy of Matter*, until finally all is absorbed into matter and all matter is engulfed in darkness.[2]

This is the ultimate solitude and hence leads to death, which is enclosed within it. Death is everywhere in *Terra Amata*, from the full-blown description of Chancelade torturing insects, through the detailed deathbed and funeral scenes of his father, to Chancelade's own death via a myriad of discussions, references, and metaphors. *Terra Amata* is the book of life against death, life in which death is incorporated, life which is merely death in another guise. The situation produces a series of war images which run through the novel, reminding us of the uncertainty of every moment. Chancelade waged war on the insects, war was in his dream, microbes make war on his body, and war is the only response man has in the face of the world he cannot understand. The situation is given concrete expression in the scene where Chancelade destroys everything he can find on a deserted beach (31–32; G 40–41) and finally in the evocation of

atomic war (206–9; G 231–34) and in the application of fallout
symptoms to the state of mankind. There are certain wars one cannot win.

V *Flight*

Chancelade cannot or will not face the void and so tries to find
some kind of solution in flight—a flight which takes a number of
forms. He tries going to bed with a woman and he tries walking
around the city, but these offer no solution. He tries to understand
also, to think and to talk "escaping as best he can, running along the
infinite roads of language" (179; G 201); but he encounters a problem presented in *The Ecstasy of Matter* already: "Thought is a void
driving into the void, you look straight in front of you and never find
anything fixed to rest on." (179; G 201) Nowhere can he escape his
destiny. He becomes more and more aware of the passing of time, of
the relativity of time according to age and circumstance. The remark
his grandmother made to him, he makes in turn to a young girl just
before his death. She said, "People don't realize it, but a life is soon
over" (76; G 89). Chancelade himself remarks, "All that, all that in
one night" (191; G 214), reminding us by his choice of words of the
whole problem of one's changing viewpoint in time and its effect on
one's sense of reality—a problem which has been considered by
Chancelade's son in relation to the movement of objects and the lack
of traces left by their passage from one place to another (131–34; G
149–52). The idea is illustrated also in Cheval Fougeux's story of his
journey in a flying saucer (148–49; G 167–68).

Man trying to escape death is playing games of a limited duration
and the ultimate game is that of trying to escape the human
condition—the game of metamorphosis. But there is no escape:
"Chancelade turned into a mouse; death turned into a cat./He
turned into a window; it turned into a stone." and the game goes on
until in desperation "He turned into a corpse, it turned into a
worm/He turned into matter, it turned into anti-matter." Everything must be swallowed up in the final combat, one reminiscent of
the struggles between magician and jinn which punctuate the *1001
Nights*. These are, of course, metaphors of Scheherezade's condition, for she is struggling against death by telling stories. Things
have come full circle, and we are back to writing as a means of
escape. LeClézio denies himself even this, for his last line is "He
turned into writing, it turned into crossing out" (180; G 202). Does

he believe in such total annihilation or is this part of the ironic tone of the volume? His answer is also in the novel: "Total is the last word. Vanished, accepted. Dead, dead. Born into a boundless life, into a life that is no longer inner nor outer, but at last, and for ever I hope, itself" (209; G 234).

VI *Ironic Tone and Structure*

Terra Amata presents a situation very similar to those we have seen before in LeClézio's fiction, but the tone of presentation is very different. The attitude is set by the preface, in which the author talks ironically about where his reader may be and why he should read this particular novel. The irony is taken up again in Chapter 23, entitled "I am dead," when we are told: "But that's enough of inventing. There is no Chancelade, there never was any Chancelade. All there ever was, was me writing these words and knowing that they hid nothing" (205; G 230). In each case the passage is followed by a long philosophical passage reminiscent of the other novels and which now, as then, seems to be being delivered seriously. The latter leads to an epilogue in the Gidean vein of "Nathanael throw my book away" and leaves the incentive in the readers' hands, for the last words of the book are: "Now it's your turn" (217; G 243). The structure is therefore very similar to that of *The Flood:* there is a philosophical section at the beginning and end of the novel and the history of the main character unrolls between them. This time, however, the philosophical sections are much shorter and they, in their turn, are surrounded by the prologue and epilogue, in which the author hardly seems to consider his books to be of great weight and moment.

The author is alternately serious and mocking of his own seriousness, not only in the basic structure but also throughout the novel. This is done primarily in two ways, one typographical and the other metaphorical.

The typographical aspect consists in breaking up the body of the text by the insertion of lists, poems, quotations in lesser known languages, and the use of different typefaces in order to change the rhythm of reading. LeClézio explains his propensity for such visual games—which we have already encountered in small numbers in the texts studied previously—in an interview at the time of the publication of *The Flood:* "I am always afraid that a book will be boring. I try to break the monotony of the writing. I attach great importance to signs: the pages of a book are a series of designs and also I am obliged to entertain myself when I write."[3]

So first there is the problem of boredom, hence, perhaps, the alternation of seriousness and games of some kind (and in *Terra Amata* one whole chapter is devoted to the many games in life). The novel has a definite ludic aspect which has a role in Chancelade's life. He plays games to fill gaps in his existence and to help time pass. (In this he reminds us of Beckett's characters in *Waiting for Godot*.) Between games the void he fears is more dangerous to him. His whole life is an oscillation between awareness of the nothingness around him and a comment on that nothingness provided by the various ludic activities in which he indulges. They create a structure to cover the mouth of a chasm. The old man Chancelade says to the girl that he has done nothing with his life and yet the alternatives he lists, "gone, to Vladivostok for instance, or got to know women, or work, or learned dozens of things. . . . I might have gone into space" (191; *G* 215)[4] are all means of flight from the void he postulates. Studies create game-type structures, journeys are means of escape and so on. Whatever he might have done would have been a game and this is recognised when the author writes: "The boy Chancelade has started to play the last game of all" (197; *G* 220).

It would seem that in LeClézio's view communication is the biggest game of all—and he plays it to the full in *Terra Amata*. First comes a long conversation between Mina and Chancelade ("Loved") which is not very striking but it is followed by Chancelade's outburst of happiness ("Happy") when he feels close to her. Immediately after this introduction to communication are four chapters which pose definite problems of comprehension for the reader. LeClézio is playing games with us this time. He is mocking our search for understanding just as he mocks that of Chancelade ("I might have . . . Sanscrit, biology, cosmography, botany, archaeology" [191; *G* 215]). In one way or another, we are all trying to grasp the life we are leading. Books offer one way—both the reading and the writing of them. LeClézio's mockery of us is a double-edged sword, for the irony turns back on himself: why does he write at all? The prologue and epilogue suddenly become warnings to himself, that he should not take what he is doing too seriously. The last paragraph of the novel explains the author's view: "What I've done I've done by chance, like a gnat in a strong wind. I've said first one thing then another. I've written pins, tobacco, passions, suffer, nylon, seed.

You've read zip-fastener, top, beauty, woman, cigarette, cloud. And accurate chance is now in motion, each speck descending into the machine along its own individual path" (217; G 243). Each of us is separate, and real communication is not possible. In this way a book becomes a series of drawings, of signs, as LeClézio suggests, and it is logical to incorporate drawings and signs of various kinds into it. If it is not possible to say anything comprehensible, it is still possible to invent a new game: "It's your turn."

This pessimism is expressed also in the major stream of metaphor which runs through the book and is present in the passage just quoted: the comparison between man and insect.

In the opening chapter ("On the earth by chance") it is suggested that the history of the world consists of the individual dramas of insects and in the following section ("I am born") the analogy between insect and human is established very clearly. Chancelade torments and kills a number of potato bugs quite gratuitously. The child is playing. The description of his actions is very detailed and realistic, but his imagination transforms the scale and tenor of his actions until he becomes their destiny. No matter what the insects may do, they spend a certain amount of time imprisoned, and then they die by some means. Their wanton destruction is recalled much later when Chancelade himself is in flight. He refers to various kinds of animals and insects, their attempts to escape, and remarks: "It's as if at the moment of the Creation there was a sly old man whose cruel laugh echoes still" (179; G 202). It is an insect that frightens Sonjia away, an insect that provides the energy for time to move on; and Chancelade refers to himself as an insect when he talks to God. And in one last irony death is described as:

> A cake that is irresistibly attractive to
> FLIES
> and FATAL
>
> (202; G 226)

The situation of man as one insect among many has been explained earlier in the novel: "So there was nothing more you could do to try to understand it. You couldn't any longer meet the terrifying glance of the absolute. You had to become an insect again, swarm on the overcrowded plateau, wave your arms, wave your legs about" (121; G 138). There was then one inevitable conclusion:

". . . play the cruel insatiable game of the insect world. . . . One day you were there. Another day you were dead. But that didn't matter at all in the moving ocean, it wasn't even tragic. It was slightly ridiculous, rather moving . . ." (121; G 138).

Death is the ultimate game, Chancelade's father played it very well. His son could never catch him peeping. Little boy Chancelade comes to watch himself die as well. His life is over. The book is over.

A final thought should be given to the lizard called Chancelade who unites many of the elements of the novel at his funeral: insects, death, games, and irony: "To my beloved lizard/ Sadly missed" (51; G 62).

CHAPTER 7

The Book of Flights

Terra Amata is an adventure in time; *The Book of Flights* is an adventure in space. *Terra Amata* is a description of the life of one man—a figure; *The Book of Flights* is a description of the ground against which the figure is visible. Hence we see that from book to book LeClézio is exploring a chain of thought. Each work follows logically from the previous one.

I *Résumé*

Young Man Hogan flees his home town and tours the world looking for an acceptable spot to stay. His journeys take him to the Mediterranean coast, the Lybian desert, then to the Far East, the Soviet Union, New York, and finally Mexico. On his way he meets a Tobagan prostitute; visits a leper colony; listens to a boy playing a flute at Angkor; watches a woman copulate with a dog; and witnesses a murder in New York. He visits some dispossessed Indians and finally finds himself in a village where everyone is blind because of the coffee fly. Interspersed between the travel episodes are passages of personal comment and the author's criticism of his own project of writing a book.

II *Masks*

In an interview with François Bott LeClézio states: "Y. M. Hogan's vice—the whole world's vice—is to remain distant and to see the world in an unusual light. . . . Y. M. Hogan is myself. I am not writing a novel. I am writing my life." Bott then asks: "Why a mask?" To which LeClézio answers: "We are all masked. We wear different masks. Young Man Hogan is a mask. LeClézio too. . . ."[1] Hogan's room has masks on the walls. He feels his room to be a prison and leaves home: "First of all pulverize one's name, one's mask. Remove the cardboard and plaster carapace, take off *one's*

81

makeup" (97; G 88). From time to time on his journey he wonders which mask to choose: "What mask to assume, what false nose, what base thought, what spurious existence? To deceive others is to get to know oneself, and vice versa" (127; G 116).

Before looking at the various lives Y. M. Hogan, alias J. M. G. LeClézio, tries, we should consider a further statement from *The Book of Flights* which puts the importance of the concept of a mask into perspective. Hogan is in Bangkok or Bang-Pa-In or Djakarta and is writing about the rhythms of life there that impose a silence upon him:

This silence from beyond words is not apathetic. This peace is not a sleep. Together, they are a rampart built against the aggressions of the sun, of noise, of war. Pride and willpower are written on the naked face of this woman standing in the center of her canoe. On her fixed mask, cast from the primordial matrix of her race, is written the text of the ancient dead whereby this people exchanged its soul with that of this piece of land. Every day, in the center of the river, this face confronts the invisible enemy. She is not aware of the fact, no one really suspects it, but this combat is joined each day, each minute, and it is a mortal combat. Is she aware of the strength and violence that animate her, when with her slow swaying movement she leans on the oar, propelling the fragile craft beneath her feet into the center of the river? She is neither aware nor unaware, for she is she, and this river is she, and each of her gestures is noble because it is not gratuitous. She describes her destiny, her civilization." (157–58; G 142–43)

The woman he describes gains strength from her mask. It is the outward expression of a way of life which is at one with its environment. The mask is part and symbol of a culture, and if Hogan refuses his mask then he refuses the civilization that produced it. This civilization he describes throughout *The Book of Flights* in terms of sun, noise, and war—the elements against which the woman needs protection. And finally he refuses it formally: "I renounce the Greco-Roman world! I am no longer its son. I can no longer be a member of its race. . . . Filthy Latin world, you wanted to make a slave out of me, so that I should kill, brand with a red-hot iron, rape in your name" (277; G 249). He refuses the Western world on the grounds that it has stolen land and culture from all around the globe and that now Western man is still killing all the others "with its airplanes, tape recorders, Bibles and vaccines" (285; G 256). This is the civilization his mask represented, the one he must escape.

III *Structure*

He escapes by fleeing as far as he can, and the novel is the story of his flight, as we have seen in the résumé above. The presentation of Hogan's journey is, however, rather complicated.

The novel breaks up into forty-four unnumbered sections of greatly varying length and contents, which are for the most part untitled. The sections fall into four major categories: (1) those which describe Y. M. Hogan's journeys and which are written in the third person; (2) those which are written in the first person and which present thoughts, meditations, opinions, states of mind; (3) five sections entitled "Self-criticism" in which the author writes in the first person about the act of writing; and (4) a small group of single pages which offer quotations, references, and, in one case, a string of insults.

The fact that LeClézio claims that he and Hogan are one and the same person (see the quotation above) simplifies the constant shift from third person to first throughout the book as it would seem that we have a consciousness (2) watching itself act (1) and commenting on its attempt to express what it sees (3). The structure of the novel expresses the distance between the world and the writer, and the grammatical forms used reinforce this division. He who acts is a long way from him who writes, except that he who acts is an actor. The last "Self-criticism" begins: "Comedian! Ham actor! It's time to bring your pantomime to a halt" (295; G 264). An actor wears a mask, and language is a mask. It is part of a culture and implies a knowledge and initiation of a life-style which must not be given away: "Language is a natural act which implies belonging. He who exists, speaks. He who does not speak, does not exist. He has no place in the world. . . . It is not enough to pronounce the syllables of the Huichol language to be Huichol. That is obvious" (282; G 253).

Hence he who deals in language wears a mask and as long as LeClézio-Hogan can write: "How to escape fiction? How to escape language?" (11; G 13) and then create a novel from the search for an answer, he is not yet free. As he writes in his "Criticism of Self-criticism": "And then, what is one to say of the writer who lies when he writes that he is lying?" (302; G 270).

The structure of the novel, therefore, reveals itself to be a triple-thickness mask (we think of the dream statues in *Terra Amata* shedding multitudes of stone faces) hiding the author from us while he is pretending to reveal himself. Is he even correct in writing "To deceive others is to get to know oneself"? It would seem that fulminations against writing in writing, a search for silence that is made up of words, and a protagonist who changes his name constantly—Jeune Homme Hogan, John Traveller, Daniel Earl Langlois, Juanito Holgazán, Young Man Hogan—are hardly likely to lead to a successful quest. In this respect the image, with which the novel opens, of the little boy watching the plane which explodes after takeoff is a splendid analogy of the whole, connecting neatly to the statement near the end of the book: "I have left my world behind, and have not yet found another. That is the tragic adventure. I have departed, but not yet arrived" (277–78; G 249).

The form of *The Book of Flights* is in itself both an escape and a prison. The author is caught in language and hence in his culture, in his mask, while making gestures to remove it. In this he is dodging the truth that he does not really wish to remove the mask or he would have stopped writing and disappeared. It is true, of course, that he will withdraw and live with the Embera Indians in Panama from 1969 to 1973, so this book is probably an early statement of the problem he will indeed attempt to solve by withdrawal from Western civilization.

LeClézio seems to have been marked by the time he spent in Bangkok and Mexico during his military service and needs to express his horror at the misery and suffering to be found in many parts of the world. The juxtaposition of city life, noise, traffic and machinery with the tranquil, self-contained dignity, poverty, and suffering of the villages is a major feature of the book. *The Book of Flights* is an outcry on a social level as well as a personal outpouring. It is, also, a literary construction, for which the author gives us his plan (186–90; G 168–71), while suggesting at the same time that he might:

> . . . scrap the idea of a plan.
> write as it comes.
> Alternate.
> Let it run out of oneself.
> Poem! Tale! Thought! Dialogue!
> ETC!

(190; G 172)

The author is certainly making himself difficult to grasp!

It is our opinion that the different sections pull against each other because they are too short and change too frequently. Also, the book is too long. Its aim could have been achieved more quickly and, thus, more successfully. The movement is held together, however, by five sequences which clarify the meaning of the whole work. These are the opening scene, in which the boy is watching the plane, the parable of Huien-Tsang, the meeting with the two flute players, and the final sequence at Belisario Dominguez. All of these passages are superb, and between them offer a progressive reduction in scope of the situation of man, his ability to flee from the void (which is, after all, the real flight with which the book is concerned) which is devastating. Hogan sees his project to find understanding reduced from an ecstatic religious pilgrimage to a sitting blindly in the dust waiting for death. Blindness is the final mask, one through which the actor cannot see.

IV *Women*

We have met blindness before in a LeClézio novel as a final image after the description of many, many pairs of eyes. Eyes have an importance in *The Book of Flights* also, this time as a means of recognizing each individual's attitude rather than as a proof of universal hostility—as they have been before. Life is again described as a war, sun and shadow have their place as does death, but none of them are as all-pervasive as in the previous novels. The leitmotiv of *The Book of Flights* is women. Women are everywhere but are always *de passage*. Hogan has no contact with any of them except Ricky the prostitute. They are there to show the multitudinousness of the world he is trying to understand, for as he remarks: "there are more women's faces than there are grains of sand" (205–6; G 184) and as he has already walked across the desert, he should know!

Women are a danger to him, bringing him nearer to death by forcing him to recognize his human condition. He writes, "This vision of the earth splitting apart . . . is within me, horribly. . . . I am fleeing to be outside myself, to be bigger than myself. I do not want to know any countries. To know is to die. I do not want to know any women. To know women is to enter the scheme of mortal things" (269; G 241). Thus, when Hogan thinks of writing to ask Laure to join him he is on the verge of accepting his death. It is amusing to recall that much earlier he has written:

"One day I shall hope to find the girl who is like this:
PROPERTY: SHE SEES AN APPLE
AND SHE THINKS THAT THE FRUIT
BELONGS TO HER BY RIGHTS
          SHE PICKS IT UP FROM THE STALL
AND EATS IT
WITHOUT THINKING
THAT THE FRUIT HAS BEEN GROWN POLISHED
          BOUGHT
          THAT IT COST MONEY
THAT IT IS FOR SALE

(128; G 116–17)

He is looking for a modern Eve who will bring mortality with her charms. Ricky and the fat woman with the dog sell their sexuality and hence belong to the city: "Town? Woman, all woman. . . . Her made-up face is an inhabited house, her body a department store" (69; G 64). They are the opposite image from that of the little native girl on the postcard Hogan will send to announce his departure, yet she exists in as many copies as they do—and she also was bought by Western technology. Hogan's escape is doomed.

V Cities

Women are compared to cities. We have seen that the women are similar and the cities Hogan visits are the same wherever he goes. Of the city he leaves originally he writes: "Town of iron and concrete, I no longer want you. I reject you. Town of valves, town of garages and sheds, I have frequented you long enough. The eternal streets hide the earth, the walls are grey screens, so are the posters and the windows. The glowing cars glide along on their tires. It is the modern world" (68; G 63). This city is just like the one that rejects him in his turn: "The cars followed each other without interruption along the road's concrete river. . . . The noise was continuous, too, and violent. . . . Above all, though, there were walls . . ." (135–36; G 123–24). Bangkok, New York, it makes little difference. They share the same anatomy:

Groin Street
Avenue of the Five Senses
Boulevard of the Femoral Arteries
Vena Cava Street
Ministry of Breasts

Pubic Garden
Larynx
Suburbs of the Anus
Sex District
Occipital Lobe Grand Theatre
   It is she, my town, my town that is all woman. Now do you understand
why I visit her so assiduously? (70; G 65)

There is a fascination, a sexual attraction, which draws Hogan to the
violence, noise, and movement of big cities. One of his descriptions
of the people passing in a street reinforces this attitude because a
number of the people listed are considered in terms of overt sexual
characteristics or of characteristics with sexual implication:

Man in shorts, scratching his genitals as he walks. . . .
Girl with bare midriff.
Girl with FLORIDA written across her bosom. . . .
Little girl throwing a box up into the air.
Woman with a target between breasts. . . .
Human cork.
Girl wearing green slacks, with the head of a doll protruding from a pocket.
(65–66; G 61)

Hogan is swallowed up in the cities, surrounded by the crowd,
unable to escape both agitation and excitement. The cities are the
result of his culture. They are Western creations wherever they may
be, and he is tied to them by his hatred. He describes them as hell,
but it is in the villages that he feels the proximity of a living death he
cannot yet accept. However, by the end he has realized that cities
are not made for people. They have a mechanical autonomy which
refuses all that is individually human. The people that are left gather
in the slums around the edges and muster what is left of themselves.
   The movement is away from the individual toward the mass, and
the description LeClézio gives of streams of traffic, crowds of
people, and miles of streets is a vast image of a spawning monster
which stretches farther and farther. LeClézio explains his attitude to
cities and to Hogan's situation in the interview already quoted:

Towns are books. Human thought is incarnate in a city as in a face. [Hence
another reason for the comparison of cities and women.] Frantically she
inscribes her mysteries in the stones of modern cities. I should like to read
all the cities of the world from end to end. If you could, you might die as a

result. . . . The individual is lost in the modern city, is lost in the community: in his kind. We are living the great adventure. The individual believes he is unique. But in a hundred years, individual thoughts will have been wiped out. It will be objects which will bear witness to our civilization: what is the thought of an individual worth compared to the waves of collective thought? I wonder if real thought doesn't reside in jukeboxes and dime-machines. Today beauty lies in Tinguely's machines. Shops are modern museums. . . . All cities are alike. Young Man Hogan tries in vain to flee: he finds the same city everywhere and everywhere he is a slave in a story which is being written inside and around him.[2]

Hogan is trapped in his culture, and all he can do is develop a consciousness of his position. This is what he is trying to do in both journey and book. He is traveling physically and mentally into new spaces and is struggling in the "Self-criticism" with the problem, value, and possibility of expressing what he has gained: the result is a threefold odyssey.

VI   *Hogan's Odyssey*

Y. M. Hogan is a name with a very Joycean ring, and *The Book of Flights* joins the list of odysseys to be found in Western literature. It is ironical that LeClézio should choose for the form of his escape one of the oldest structures of the culture he wishes to leave.

Hogan can be identified with Odysseus and has his Penelope in Laure, the girl whom he left at home, his Calypso and his Circe in Ricky and the Japanese woman. Like Odysseus he has left behind him a state of war epitomized in the description of a bus: "It zigzags, it spits from the machine gun's barrel and its bullets ricochet explosively from the walls, smash into human flesh and open up little stars of blood. The heavy machine gun fires upon the crowd . . ." (71–72; *G* 66); and, like Odysseus, he finds danger wherever he goes. Also like the Greek, he travels much of the time by boat.

In the *Odyssey* the landfalls are of two kinds—arrival on other kings' territory, where the danger may be acute but is the usual treatment given to an intruder, and landing on the shores of a country ruled by an immortal. In the latter situation the danger is unexpected and unknown, and the lesson learned has, as a result, greater significance.

It would seem reasonable to make a similar distinction in the case of Y. M. Hogan's journeys. The cities would fit into the first category of aggression on a human scale which can be overcome or more

usually appeased. Hogan and Ulysses often think of settling down in
the various places they stay and always live to move on.

In the second category, for Hogan, are the villages: the one on the
island in the river where all is quiet and beautiful, Shark Island in
the Bay of California and Belisario Dominguez. These are the Lotos
lands, where all seems serene and tranquil, where a traveler is
tempted to put aside the bustle, violence, and noise of his previous
existence and to sit quietly until death. But in each case there is a
danger lurking: the first island is a leper colony; the second is inaccessible already and leaves those who have been there in a paralysis
of nostalgia; the third causes blindness.

In each case the traveler must be prepared to sacrifice some part
of himself—to be maimed—in order to achieve peace. And this
Hogan will not accept.

The choice between city and village is like that between Scylla
and Charybdis. Whichever Hogan chooses he is risking his life.
Whichever way he goes someone will die.

The flute player at Angkor has the role of the Sirens. The music
the little boy creates has the same quality of drawing man out of the
world:

. . . one immediately understood that it was an inexhaustible melody.
Nothing began it, nothing could stop it. (160–61; G 145)

It [the flute] did not search the soul, it did not try to convince. It was there,
there only when it had to be. . . . (162; G 147)

It [the music] sucked things up from the world, dissolved them gently,
made them disappear. . . .

It was the voice of a woman, perhaps, . . .The voice, in a sense, of eternal
woman. . . . She invaded space, she covered the earth. Wherever one
looked she was there. . . . (163; G 147)

It [the music] formed an integral part of everything. . . . There was no
longer any reason to listen. Or to be far away. One no longer had ears. One
was close, face to face with it. . . .

The ductile notes had turned into a true gaze, a long gaze of awareness
that lingered over the countryside. . . . (163; G 148)

With a single leap it had attained the limits of the real world, had passed
through existence like a shiver. . . . It had travelled . . . farther than
knowledge, farther than the dizzy spiral in the process of boring its way into
a madman's skull. (164; G 148)

When the music stops Hogan feels that the whole world is unin-habited. The sirens paint a picture of their world which tempts man and deprives him of his reason. He who hears seeks farther and farther for what he thinks he heard—even though, like Hogan, he cannot remember what indeed it was the music taught him.

VII   A Zen Journey

The other flute player, the one at Cuzco, and Hogan's walk across the desert belong to the second Odyssey. This is a mental journey which traces Hogan's changing attitude to the world. It is a change which it is difficult for him to make because of the seething multi-plicity of the world which surrounds and tempts him. He is struggl-ing with this world for most of the book, but the direction in which he is moving is clearly indicated.

First there is a story which illustrates his situation and indicates what he must do. This is the parable of Huien-Tsang, the Zen master who dies in the desert. At this stage Hogan is in the position of the disciple to whose question, "Master, when shall we reach our goal?" the master replies, "It is not the unknown, since it is the path of Buddha. It is not silent, since we have the word of Buddha. Why should you be afraid to die, since it is the life of Buddha?" (110; G 100). The disciple runs away back to civilization—to the city—and Hogan is carried out of the desert in a truck. Meanwhile, the master goes blind and crawls on the stumps that are left of his legs to achieve the life he has lost.

The three stages of the master's suffering which brings him to death, namely, blindness, stumps for limbs, and nostalgia, are the three states of man in the villages described above and through which Hogan must pass despite himself. These have already been suggested in the titles of books Hogan picks up in the first city he visits: *A Nose for Trouble* (leprosy), *The Tragedians* (the Kunkaak Indians), and *Lord of the Flies* (Belisario Dominguez). (The films [listed on 76; G 70, 193] are applicable to the cities. *The Woman of the Dunes* links the two parts of Hogan's quest as Huien-Tsang is linked to ". . . the army of the desert's women with their long piercing sobs. And these supernatural voices drew him towards them" [118; G 107]. This is the action the city women have on Hogan. The film was made in Tokyo and Hogan goes there.)

Hogan tries to obstruct someone studying Zen by posing the

problem of the physical world (124; G 113), but a little later there is a long passage in which the situation and reasoning is that of a Zen disciple. Hogan has realized that he was asking the wrong kind of questions: "The only questions I used to ask myself were unimportant, irrelevant ones, like: Is there a God? . . . They were bad questions because it was obvious that I couldn't answer them" (167; G 151). He goes on to explain that the reason he asked such questions is that language has made him accustomed to formulating things explicitly—that is, explicitly, according to linguistic reasoning. Language thus imposes limitations on man's thinking by requiring him to express his thought in words.

Hogan has got as far as realizing that "it is a matter of conceiving of the several" (168; G 152), but his problem is that he still believes there are questions to be asked. The comment on his attitude lies immediately before his meditation: "Those who follow ignorance enter into the darkness of the blind, but those who seek only knowledge enter into an even greater darkness"[3] (166; G 150).

We see that the state Hogan must achieve is described by the flute player at Cuzco if we realize that we should draw an analogy between the music and the way man should live his life: "It was the melody of a fugue relieved of all its useless noises. Become pure. Stripped of all the humming, become the simple breath of a man who has no desire to describe the world, who has no desire to imitate the wind or the rain, who no longer has anything to do with the real. True respiration which utters its little cries, which raises its taut stems in the transparent air, which is itself, magnificently itself, itself for itself, the essence of itself" (291; G 261). No more questions, no more descriptions, no more words, just a simple acceptance of life for itself in the present, free from the noise of the world within which the person lives. Hogan is fleeing, both away from this and toward it at the same time. His view of the world as a "*CUL ETERNEL DE SAC*" (293; G 263) is perhaps the nearest he has come to accepting the death which he as been trying to avoid by constant movement and, above all, by a constant flow of language, which keeps him prisoner in a limit cultural framework.

Hogan-LeClézio's final obstacle is, therefore, that he must come to terms with his need to express both his thoughts and his experiences in words. Thus we arrive at the third path through *The Book of Flights*—that offered by the comments on writing.

VIII *"Self-criticism"*

Here we encounter immediately the idea of masks with which we began. We are told that an author chooses masks behind which he hides to justify his work when, in fact, this work is useless. Yet in decrying the necessity of another novel, is the author not creating still another excuse? Is he sneering at his own uncontrollable need to write or is he playing a game with us? "It is not sufficient to hurl abuse at literature. That must be done with something other than words. Abandon one's conscious self, disappear into the world. Become a Martian" (127; G 116), he writes and then proceeds to play word games with what he should do. He would seem to be stuck on the horns of a dilemma which he is not about to resolve. In the third "Self-criticism" we read: "I wanted to flee by going farther than myself. I wanted to visit countries where no one speaks, countries where it is the dogs that write novels, not men in horn-rimmed glasses. . . . I wanted to write too . . ." (186; G 168), and at the end of the same section we find the statement: "I do not hate you. I simply want to understand you. I do not want to find the truth. I simply want to tell you that you are not dead. . . . Filthy, filthy writer living off his feelings like a whore off her flesh. I'm saying all this out of spite" (191; G 172).

The split resolves itself somewhat in the final section, for there we learn that LeClézio-Hogan makes an important distinction between writing and talking, for example, which shows that he thinks writing is artificial. He hates writing because it deforms what he wants to express. He despises writers for living within that prison: "What remains true, and constant, is writing's abandonment of reality, loss of meaning, logical madness" (264–65; G 236)." . . . I wish I wrote the way one speaks. I wish I wrote the way one sings, or the way one yells. . . . But that is simply not done. So I write the way one writes. . . . Behind all the papers, behind all the photos, there is a universe which I know well and which I am never able to rediscover" (265; G 237). And yet he is pleased to have that separation between him (the writer) and himself (the observed consciousness) and the world. In writing novels he accepts his flight from direct contact with the world, accepts his lack of spontaneity: "I was not capable of sending you the post-cards at the right moment" (267; G 239); but he acknowledges his need to express himself: "So how could I possibly say what is meant by misery, or love, or fear?

Perhaps people write novels simply because they do not know how to compose letters, or vice versa" (267; G 239).

All would be well and LeClézio's frankness is touching until he adds "or vice versa." His sincerity is suddenly in question once again and *The Book of Flights*, which was becoming an honest book constructed from a flight (LeClézio's) as well as a book full of flights (Hogan's), suddenly produces another one and eludes our grasp once more. What we thought was a face proves to be yet another mask, which leads us on to the author's designation of himself as an actor—an actor who does not know how to leave the stage: "Man as intellectual, eager to get to know things so as to be able to construct his systems. Man as comedian, eager to forget the world so as to make a witty remark" (301; G 269). We return to the division between expression and world to-be-expressed and the original idea of making novels without words.

IX *Conclusion*

At one point in *The Book of Flights* there is a definition of flight which incorporates all three levels of flight that have been discussed in this chapter: "Flight is not silence. It is, all of a sudden, an avalanche of noises compounded of rustlings, creakings, murmurs. Flight means talking, no longer with the aim of being understood, but so as to make a noise, one more noise among all the others. . . . Flight can never be solitude. Rather it means finding oneself unexpectedly in the incredible crowd with its whirlwinds of movements" (240–41; G 215). Nonflight is acceptance of solitude like that of Huien-Tsang, acceptance of silence, acceptance of death. *The Book of Flights* is a manual of the ways to run away from man's condition—a condition LeClézio has described so poignantly in his earlier works.

CHAPTER 8

War

WAR has been an evermore frequently recurring image in the works of LeClézio and it would perhaps be useful to consider its previous significances before beginning a study of *War* itself.

I   *War in* The Flood

The Flood is the first novel in which war plays an important role. The book opens with an ambiguous but threatening statement: "At the beginning. . . . Everything began to grow dark, objects took on a regular pattern, lapped scales like thin blades of steel or chain mail, that frittered away what little brightness still remained. Other objects, themselves sources of light . . . overwhelmed by the vast proportions of some ill-defined yet imminent happening made ridiculous by the mere fact of comparison with this enemy (as it were) against whom they had to sally forth and do battle" (1; G 9) War is imminent between the forces of light and darkness. This war is symbolized by Besson's game of a battle between blacks and whites (129; G 125), and it reaches a conclusion in the appeal to speak out against atomic war at the end of the novel. Light and darkness are the sun and the black sun—the black sun being the image of malefic heat and light and therefore a metaphor for atomic warfare, which is the product of modern civilization and hence to a certain extent already its representative: "Do you realise that every year the world spends sixty billion francs cold currency on weapons of destruction? Do you realise that one hundred million men and seventy per cent of the world's scientists are employed on war production?" (289; G 273). The fear, at the moment, is concentrated in real war, but the elements of evolution are present in the language LeClézio uses. Here we find a call for response, for reaction, and a comment on what the author expects to receive:

YOU'RE WRONG, IT IS NOT POINTLESS, AND IT IS VERY MUCH
YOUR BUSINESS
BECAUSE YOU HAVE THE RIGHT TO LIVE
If you are on your own, no-one will hear you. BUT YOU ARE NOT ON
YOUR OWN.
"Jessie James: Hopeless Blues" (289; G 273)

II *War in* Terra Amata

In *Terra Amata* the theme is taken up again and has a more
frequent place in the novel. There are several conversations concerning World War II. Chancelade dreams about war (59; G 71). His
dreams are all concerned with life as a perilous enterprise, so that
the war dream takes meaning from its context even though there is
no direct link between life and war in the passage itself. There are
connections elsewhere in the novel however, and they deal with life
on various levels. There is the war the body wages constantly on
bacteria in order to stay alive from minute to minute (161; G 182),
and previous to this state there is the idea of birth itself as a war in
which the child fights the adult for a place in the world:

It was no use trying to escape or to forget: it was a total war, without
mercy. Every second a new body was born somewhere on earth, pushing an
old body into the abyss. They were everywhere: these dwarfs with men's
and women's faces spied on you ceaselessly from gardens, out of car windows, from behind trees or from the shadows. They listened. They continually stole your thoughts, your words, your acts, your passions. They ate your
food, breathed your air, they even went off with your wives.

But after all it was not really so unfair . . . like them you had killed in
order to live. (128–29; G 146)

This idea is continued in *The Book of Flights* by the story of Daniel
Earl Langlois and his friend Tower who plan to take over the world
(216; G 195).

The major image is the one which is created in terms of an
analogy—that of Chancelade killing insects with the destruction of a
city—and which ends with the total annihilation of a real city—
Hiroshima. Let us consider the two passages for a moment. Both are
too long to quote in full.

Chancelade creates a city but the inhabitants do not behave as he wishes: "He looked at the town with hatred. . . . They'd rebelled. They'd refused the kingdom he'd offered them and hadn't wanted him as their only god. For that they would know his vengeance. He was going to kill them all without exception" (16; G 24). The city he had offered was a metal grid from a doorstep. Hence each insect had an identical rectangular space in which to exist. There was nowhere for him to go but into another rectangle and not enough room to move freely. This is the life the insects refused to adapt to—and in *Terra Amata* insects are always used symbolically to describe the human condition. Hence we have an early description of a modern city with some kind of a god who demands acceptance from the inhabitants of all change of their life pattern that he may care to impose.

In *Terra Amata* it is the element of destruction that is taken up again in a passage on the atomic bomb, which is much more developed than the mention in *The Flood*. Here the bomb has been dropped: "The world is coming to an end, it is on its deathbed. Suddenly on the surface of the earth the great dome of light has exploded like a volcano. . . . And that was the last crime of my life, the greatest and most terrible of all. I didn't say anything, I didn't do anything, I was just there in the dazzling circle that spread out over the earth, the circle of my intelligence and my hatred. It was the last of my wars, the one I didn't wage alone, the one that everyone waged with me" (206; G 230–31).

"The world is coming to an end in this ball of fire. Beyond, there is nothing. After this futile moment *in which one rather unimportant person is undone*, it is the end of the universe made visible; the fated end of ages and ages of civilization, of hope, literature, love and faith" (208; G 232–3; my italics). We see that what has been destroyed is a way of life; it is the world as it had been throughout civilization, the world in which each individual man, his thoughts, his feelings, his beliefs mattered to everyone else. In Hiroshima a city was destroyed in the way an anthill is exterminated or as Chancelade massacres his insects. At least Chancelade gave names to his insects so that they could be remembered for their sacrifice: "And so died Antis, Goliath, Vélo, Ajax, Potato and Bug, sole survivors of the great massacre that took place that day among the potato-bugs" (19; G 27) The age of individual names which help man to know and understand his environment is over. A new age of new names, each of which encompasses a diversity of objects, is born. *The Book of Flights* has none of the lists of names of friends and acquaintances we find in the earlier books. Instead, it has descriptions of unknown passersby, lists of products, producers, and generalities:

men!
jelly fishes!
eucalyptus!
green-eyed women!
Bengali cats!
pylons!
cities!
springs!
green plants, yellow plants!

(10; G 12)

We are in the age of categories, of similarities, of mass production.

III   *War in* The Book of Flights

The war is more obvious now. Instead of being an accident which most people can avoid or ignore, it is everywhere, everyday in very ordinary things. Man must realize this and fight.

In *The Book of Flights* war is in the city. We have already quoted the passage describing a bus p. 88 above. We are told again: "The vehicles had won their war. They were there, lording it over the country they had conquered with their steel breastplates and rubber wheels. . . . They were charged with menace. . . . They wanted to kill him [Young Man Hogan]" (248–49; G 222–23). This war is against objects, against a situation which is changing and only a stable culture can protect one against such peril. (See above p. 82 for the description of the Thai woman in her boat.)

Young Man Hogan runs away from cities because that is where the battles are being fought. Before he leaves on his journey he makes a statement which clarifies his desire to escape:

THE WORLD IS MODERN   RAPTURE OF MECHANISMS
                             OF ELECTRICITY
                             OF AUTOMATONS

Modern world: rapture of metals and glass walls.
Pale are the walls

Pale
the broad concrete brows
facing the ocean of sound and light.
It is war, calm war
being fought with wielded lines and curves.
War between plastics and linoleum
between neon nylon and dralon®
The war of savage mouths.
Today
the armies have burrowed inside the walls
beneath their hard boots the ground shakes
and the air quivers.
The are modern
They are called
SUBSIDIZED BUILDING PROJECT, AUTOROUTE DU SUD
TURNPIKE, TORRE DE AMERICA LATINA
HIKARÍ TRAIN
KODAMÁ TRAIN
MAFEKING SEMENT MAATSKAPPIJ BEPERCK
Those really are their names.
They boast these extraordinary retractile names
They have fingernails, hooks, knives and fists
They have silver breastplates
Wide white blocks and black bars against the sky
From their throats emerge the mysterious cries
FISSURE FISSURE
LIGHTNING FLASH
(Prrfuitt-clack!
BOM! BODOM!)
    Highways bridges parking lots
    Snowy buildings
    Deserts, o deserts!
They strike, and their straggering blows
arouse a sweet rapture.
They tear asunder
opening wounds that do not bleed but smile with pleasure.
They crush beneath their four black tyres
and trace on the skin the path's secret
the spirit of the war against death
all the zigzags of the century unconscious of its identity.

                                        (120–21; G 109–10)

The war is against death—death of the individual caused by his
being overwhelmed by a mass of man-made objects against which
his culture offers no protection.

IV *War*

The contents of *War* comes, now, as no surprise. LeClézio has prepared us for it at length. Bea B. and Mr. X are in the situation of the soldiers on the Plateau of Stones in *The Book of Flights* (270–74; *G* 242–46), fighting battles against the forces of the establishment— the individualists, the guerillas, the heroes who are destined to die.

V *Résumé*

Bea B. and her friend Mr. X study life in a modern city in order to understand it and wage war upon it. They watch the traffic on the turnpike, go to the airport, and lie on the runway while a DC 8 takes off over them. Bea B. spends time in a department store, studying a crossroads, and in a dance hall at night. She is fascinated by the city and aware of its beauty. Little by little she learns to deal with machines and is able to create legends for this new world she is in. One day she is picked up by people in a big American car who go on a man hunt and kill a pedestrian. Mr. X curses the world and threatens a new Apocalypse. Bea sees signs of their victory in the city but is equally aware of the signs of war: a garbage truck, a wreckers yard, and a concentration camp. Finally she loses herself in the crowd in the subway and rides away.

VI *Bea B. and Mr. X*

These two characters in whose name and voice *War* is written are Everywoman and Everyman, as their names indicate: Bea B = B. A. B., the first letters of the alphabet turning in on themselves, and, of course, it is unnecessary to comment on "Mr. X." The names are presumably chosen to show both the loss of individuality against which they are struggling and also the universality of their situation. All of this is reinforced by the fact that we know very little concerning either of them: Bea has a grandmother and a brother, Mr. X a motorcycle. Neither of them has any fixed frame of reference, a job, for example, nor are they constant in relation to each other. Mr. X and B. A. B. are any man and any woman in the street who may or may not know each other (indeed Bea is often referred to simply as "the girl"). Hence in one section Bea B. will see a passerby X, in the following one she will be out with Mr. X, at another moment he can die and then she can meet him again—all of which occurs in *War*.

Together, that is, as two human beings, they work together in the war effort. Others are with them—for example, THE INVINCIBLE ARMADA (255; *G* 256)—in the battles against a synthetic world;

and they find signs both of war and of victory wherever they go. Bea
B. finds an important one on a parking lot:

It was a really extraordinary drawing, I assure you, such a beautiful drawing
that I shall never forget it. . . . It sounds silly, saying it now, but I looked at
it without a thought in my mind, just with the strange sort of emotion one
would feel when listening to some very beautiful piece of music wafting out
of the night. . . . The drawing was like the sun, spreading the rays of its
rudimentary arms and legs across the ground. At the top, two semi-circles
with a dot in the center of each one. Lower down, another dot, barely
visible. Then, between the two curves of the wide thighs, a sex like an open
eye, and a vertical phallus pressing against it. No face, no soul, no feeling,
nothing, only this symbol of action, this diagram that captured the whole of
life. (253; G 254)

The drawing is a gesture, the action is a gesture (and it is linked
here to writing which is given the same end), a gesture of affirmation
of life in its simplest form. It is a recognition of the past, during
which the goddess of love was revered, whatever her name may
have been in any given time and place, and also a symbol of each
individual whose need to escape solitude and whose need to take a
place in the continuous chain of human life is encapsulated in the
sex act: "Just a sign that said what had to be said, without flourishes:
here I am, I exist, I want something out of life" (254; G 255). The
same idea is expressed in a later section in which we see Bea B.
running away from a car, running into a city which offers no haven.
The car is transformed into a man who catches her and takes / rapes
her while the city collapses about their ears and Bea B. has a vision
of peace in the future (256–63; G 257–66). Her orgasm is again an
affirmation of human relations and feelings, a sign of victory over the
city; but the fear and violence of the act itself are an expression of
the war which is in Mr. X and which he puts into her. The scene
which comes near the end of the novel is a symbol of their rev-
olutionary activity.

It is also a repeat of events in the life of Adam Pollo and François
Besson and as such would suggest that LeClézio sees the relations
between the sexes as a war also. The presentation of Bea B. and Mr.
X is certainly made from a particular male viewpoint. Bea B. is lost
in the modern world. She takes all her directives from Mr. X,
practicing assiduously whatever he asks her to do. She seems to fall
in love with him, at which point the whole city is transfigured and
she appreciates its beauty (139–56; G 140–57). Mr. X becomes a god

to whom she is totally submissive even when he abandons her—his death in this context is symbolic as she meets him in the street later, and the rape is the image of the power he has over her. *War* could be read as the story of a love affair.

VII *Womankind*

Bea B. is the first female protagonist that LeClézio has created, but as we have seen he undermines her by subordinating her to the anonymous male. This is, however, only one element of the ambiguous presentation of woman in *War*. On the one hand there is the girl who is pretty, tends to wait at bus stops a lot, and is fighting the war in the shape of Bea B. On the other hand there is the symbol of war—the woman of advertising campaigns and billboards: ". . . exquisitely beautiful, utterly desirable women, giant woman standing naked against the walls and the rivers of sperm will never rise high enough to cover them. Alien women with metallic bodies and white hair and long slim legs sheathed in fishnet stockings" (236; *G* 237).

Here sex is being used by the enemy no longer as a sign of human life but as a weapon in the war of objects. It is part of a movement to transform people into identical objects and, at the same time, into ideal consumers. And the result is slowly being achieved:

One day, by chance, I saw this woman. . . . I sensed that this woman was the war's figure-head, gliding safely through the scenes of battle while slaughter raged around her. Her water-repellent skin was moulded to her flesh like a breastplate. . . . She is called Bea B., or else, Beauty Lane. . . . Perhaps the war's mechanism is still inside her body, perhaps it could be torn out. . . . She must be stopped! Her skin must be stripped off and air and water allowed to filter through her body. But the air is absent and the water is imprisoned within pipes and taps. (227–28; *G* 228)

Woman is here seen as a collaborator who must be saved from herself—and the rape scene gains yet another dimension.

Women are attributed the power to stop the war but will not because they are fascinated by the objects around them. Woman is shown as the ultimate consumer.

VIII *Objects*

The temples, of which woman is the goddess, are the department store and the supermarket, and the treasures on display in these temples are primarily prepacked foods, such as those in the photographs accompanying the text. Bea B. is attracted by a tin of sardines for example:

The supermarket was ablaze with the light of two hundred neon tubes as she entered and walked very quickly between the display shelves. She saw terrible things, very soft objects in satin cases, violent objects, silent objects, objects that had no name. She picked them up then put them down again. There was a huge nylon basket filled with thousands of rectangular boxes fashioned from polished tin, with a picture painted on one side, and the words written in black letters:

SARDINES IN OLIVE OIL
COMAC S.A.
MOROCCO

She took the cold smooth tin, the beautiful oblong sculpture, and she thought that nothing so beautiful had been made for centuries, and that nothing remotely resembling it would ever be made again. . . . /The girl busied herself with things like this as she fled through the city, to keep fear at bay. (169–70; G 171; my italics)

Objects are solid, can be held firmly, possessed, and hence protect the people who own them to a certain extent from the fear that Bea B. explains as: "A low noise, a tremor, a peculiar rustling sound as though there were termites gnawing away everywhere" (187; G 188). But while protecting a person temporarily from fear they also prevent thought and understanding; they thus produce the type of woman described above who is born (in Bea B.'s new story of Creation) "emerging one day from her brand-new nylon sack, with sleek skin and hair and breasts and belly . . ." (195; G 197) in order to walk in front of shop windows.

The proliferation of consumer goods is a danger, then, a major element in the war—which LeClézio views as a violent struggle to protect each individual's thoughts from the constant assault of identical merchandise and the torrents of words connected to it. Mr. X defines the situation in his Apocalyptic denunciation of the modern world:

Ceaselessly, night and day, they are born: tinned pineapple, tinned ham, fruit, vegetables, perfumes in their little square bottles, Onyx, Tabac, Arpège. . . . All this wealth is spread out there in front of me, and their glitter dazzles my eyes! . . . All shining with their fierce power. . . . I walk through the labyrinth filled with facile mysterious objects. I pass through clouds of silver. . . . The world is offering its own blood for sale! . . .

The end is near. . . . Human knowledge is not so vast as the number of objects offered to its scrutiny; the number of words is vaster than language itself. Thought, limitless thought, stretches in all directions. The most secret dreams are marked out perfectly clearly, perfectly visible. The mysteries are not inner mysteries. . . . For all these things are happening on the surface. . . .

. . . The reservoir of substance is immense, frontierless, existing from all eternity. Objects create those that create them: then they kill them. (229–30; G 229–31)

The world is about to collapse under a proliferation of everything— under the number of people and the things they make.

Objects are, therefore, presented as the enemy of the mind and soul of man. Cars are the enemy of his body. Cars are the horsemen of this new Apocalypse. They have taken over the world— LeClézio devotes pages of description to roads, crossroads, and vehicles—and urge man to destroy himself. They hypnotize him until he steps under their wheels, or they hunt for him actively and run him down (197–215; G 199–216).

The war is total. It is for the survival of man in the teeth of the environment he has created.

IX *Structure*

As in the Apocalypse, there are seven stages in Bea B.'s initiation: the turnpike, a department store, a crossroads, a nightclub, a highrise building, an airport and runway, and finally the cars on the boulevard. In between these experiences, which are reported in the third person about Bea B., someone who also seems to be Bea but who resembles all the other LeClézio heroes as well talks in the first person about fear, the world, and the war and occasionally writes in a little notebook. She is trying desperately to understand what is going on and believes that somewhere out there is a plan of the war that she can find, or a word that will stop the war just like magic. While she is looking for these she walks around the city as did her predecessors.

The city again seems to be Nice, especially identifiable by the airport on the seashore. It is understandable to anyone who knows the city why cars should turn into such a nightmare for anyone who

lives there; for wide boulevards have been torn through the heart of
a city ill-equipped to bear the resulting traffic load. The noise is
all-engulfing.

War has no plot and its storyline follows Bea B.'s psychological
reaction to her situation—that is, to the world in which she finds
herself. The novel is not divided into conventional chapters but falls
into sections creating this pattern:

I   Prologue: war
II   Bea B.'s need for a new life, for solitude
      She calls on Mr. X for help
      They decide to fight
      Fear, possible flight, and ways of fighting
      Experiences: turnpike, jukebox, shop, crossroads
      Bea B. sees the whole city as part of the war
III   A personal history of war. *Mr. X writes a letter to Bea*
      Bea B. and Mr. X talk about their childhood fears, etc.
      Bea B. is happy
      Bea writes to Mr. X about the need to express oneself
IV   More experiences
      Bea B. fascinated now, not afraid
      She recounts the new Creation
      Death ride
V   Mr. X's curse
VI   Victory signs
      Bea B.'s orgasm/rape/dream
      War, signs
      Bea's disappearance
VII   Epilogue: war

Like this outline the novel falls into seven parts. It is our
Apocalypse! There is a balance between the movement in Part 2
from fear to an awareness of total war and the advance in Part 4 from
fascination of death; while Part 3 provides both a lull and an analogy
between the soldier's experience and that of someone struggling
through life—both needing to express the danger that surrounds
them. We have discussed the significance of the rape scene already;
thus the reason for its position between signs of victory and of war is
clear.

Mr. X's curse is inevitable after all that has gone before, especially
after Bea B.'s recounting of the new world with its myths of the first
cigarette, the black car, Monopol, and the packaged woman. First

Creation, then death (the man who was hunted down), then Apocalypse once more, with the inevitable death of Mr. X counterbalancing that of the pedestrian and echoing that of the soldier shot in the back (128; G 129).

Mr. X's life cycle is very like that of Christ even to having "a large red gash in the left side" (123; G 123). He is unknown , ignored except by those who believe in his message of a war to fight and a better world to win. He preaches the downfall of the kingdoms of the world in very biblical language (quoting the prophet Jeremiah); he is killed; and he leaves his disciples instructions to carry on his work before rising again (Bea sees him in the street). In such a context Bea's sexual experience becomes a mystical one.

As we have already suggested, it is possible, also, to consider *War* in terms of the story of a sexual relationship in the modern world. The structure described above holds good, and it is certainly true that there is a definite sexual thread running through the work.

All aspects of the story, all possible readings, as well as reminder links with the previous novels are provided by the quotations which head each of the sections which deals with Bea B. in the third person. Each quotation comments on the section it heads, and the scope ranges from classical authors of the Orient and the Occident to contemporary scientists and writers. The quotations provide a résumé of the novel, emphasize its main themes and images, and comment on the situation in which the characters find themselves. The modern city is as devastating, at least to LeClézio, as many products of science fiction.

X *Conclusion*

It remains only to comment on the prologue and epilogue, since there seems to be a definite shift of position from the one to the other which is not really accomplished by the bulk of the text. The novel begins with the statement that "War has broken out. Where or how, nobody knows any longer. But the fact remains"; and it adds, "Nobody will survive unscathed" (7; G 7). The war has developed from a knowledge of evil and evil is "IMMENSELY EXTERNAL. . . . The evil—the war—is to have imagined the external. Then, having imagined it, to have opened the doors of the internal. The delicate substance has leaked out . . . something had disappeared, had withdrawn from the core of all beings" (14–15; G 14–15); and in that hollow war grows. As LeClézio writes elsewhere in the novel: "It's the words inside me struggling to fight against the words outside, and they are going to lose the battle" (187; G 188).

The epilogue, on the other hand, begins unexpectedly: "The world has begun. Nobody knows where, or how, but the fact remains that it has just come into being" (283; G 284). Since we know that birth is war, we realize that the beginning and the end of the novel are saying the same thing; what is surprising to learn however, is that the catastrophe is permanent, that war *is thought* rather than a defense of thought; thus, wanting to understand the war becomes a turning in upon one's own consciousness in the desire to understand thought—the story does not lead to this.

It is perhaps better to consider *War* in less rigorous terms, to accept it as a poem of the modern city. The text is a cry of love and hatred, attraction and repulsion, touched with black humor from time to time, from the heart of an author who is not at all comfortable in his relations with either people or physical environment. Above all it is a condemnation of our society and the way we are letting it treat us. *War* is our epic.

CHAPTER 9

The Indian Texts

IN the period between *War* (1970) and *The Giants* (1973) LeClézio wrote three books: a volume on art entitled *Haï* (1971), a text on the effects of hallucinogenic drugs, *Mydriase* (1973), and a book called *Au Pays d'Iwa (In Iwa's Country)*. The latter was announced by Gallimard but withdrawn before publication by the author who felt that his text would be a travesty of experience he was trying to transmit—that of the life of the Embera Indians in Panama—a betrayal of the teaching he had received and also a blatant manifesta-. tion that either he had not understood or had refused whatever knowledge had been offered him. As neither of these states of mind were applicable to his case, LeClézio would not release the manuscript. Only one extract definitely from the text is available; some thirty-four pages, were published in *Les Cahiers du Chemin* under the title "Le Génie Datura" ("The Spirit Datura").[1]

As far as we can tell *In Iwa's Country* would have developed the native village side of *The Book of Flights* and thus provided a counterbalance to *War*, with *Haï* creating a link between the two. We are reduced, here, to a discussion of *Haï* and the drug texts, since they are all that LeClézio has chosen to reveal of the years he spent living in the Panamanian forest.

I Haï

In *Haï* we find perhaps the clearest statement of the beliefs LeClézio has been putting forward in his fiction. He seems to find definite support for his own attitudes in the state of mind and way of life of Central American Indians and the support he finds provides examples to illustrate, and render more accessible, what has been until now his private vision. The author is very much aware of this and begins his book: "I don't really know how this is possible, but it

is so: I am an Indian. I did not know I was before I met Indians . . ."
(p. 7)

II *Résumé of* Haï

The text is concerned with the contrast between the Indians' use
of language, music, and art in their culture and the way the arts fit
into the Western world. In brief, for the Indian, language, music,
and painting are functions in life and natural expressions of life
which are recreated at moments of need by each and every individual. There is no hierarchy of talent, no specialization, no isolation
of works created. In the West it is quite the contrary. Artists are set
apart, their works are not incorporated into the daily life of their
civilization and, above all, are not the natural and continuous expression of a shared way of life. At best each work is a function of its
creator's existence, at worst it is a quest for fashion and fame. The
true manifestations of the West are commercial art and popular
music, which are the product of and have an effect on the daily
habits of the masses—of the tribe.

III *Energy*

Haï, which means energy, offers a confrontation of the ways by
which certain psychic energies are expended by the Indians and by
the white races. The Indian uses the human skills of language,
music, and painting, to learn to know his world and to concentrate
his vital forces in such a way that he can go beyond ordinary knowledge. In the West these forces are dissipated by excess exposure to
and use of these same skills. We remain scuttling around the surface
of our life, buffeted by words against which we have no protection.
LeClézio writes:

Towns, mechanical societies, large groups of men, agglomerations of buildings, scientific diagrams, and dictionaries. . . . Listen to them, they say:
progress, history, conquest of the universe. They say: man's end is in man,
the reasons for language are language itself. Towns do not leave us enough
time to know. They have laid their traps, woven their snares of cause and
effect. . . . One of the tricks of the towns is making us believe they are
eternal. They want to let us think that they are the culmination of natural
civilizations, that they explain them. (15–16)

This is what he has been illustrating in his novels with the response which is also stated clearly here: "So, what you find out one day, just like that, simply by sitting on a rock by the sea, you see, is that human experience is included in the universe's experience. That means that language is an expression of the universe modified by men's mouths, a language which is interpreted, so to speak, and whose original will always remain untranslated" (15).

This the Indian understands. In him there is no war. War is born of the need to understand, in a way that can be expressed in words, the world in which the individual exists. It is the search for the secret of the universe. It is the belief that there is something to be sought and found which is the key to life—a belief, in fact, that there is something which can be possessed, just as a can of sardines can be possessed.

Western art is a taking possession bit by bit of everything around it—an occupation, a transposition into a systematized form which can then be analysed in words. Labeled and defined, the world will eventually belong to Western man. But the world is not easy to grasp: "The world does not want to talk, it has a horror of knowledge. It does not want language, it is not at all interested in words" (21). To describe the world is to reduce it to man's measure. The Indian knows that this is ridiculous. He knows that language cannot control the world for man; rather, it reveals man's self to the world in all his vulnerability. (Something or someone else might learn his language and hence trap him as the Indian traps birds and animals by imitating their calls.) Thus:

If he distrusts language, expression, it is because he is conscious of the dangers inherent in them. Spoken language is not only a means of communication with the world; indeed, it can be a betrayal, an exposure of oneself. Language is closed. It is held in common by the tribe or race. It is an act which is not gratuitous and which cannot be unconscious. Speech is the property of men, the affirmation of their existence. Just like the major actions affirming life, birth, copulation, childbirth, death, language is magic. That is to say, a pact associating man and the universe. (34–35)

Western man does not use his language properly because he is not in a proper relationship with his world: "In creating towns, inventing concrete, tarmacadam and glass, men have invented a new jungle whose inhabitants they have not yet become. Perhaps they will die before they recognize it" (41). The Indian accepts his world and is accepted by it. There is no aggressive desire for mastery such as that between automobile and man that we have seen in *War*. The Indian knows that there is no secret to be discovered and owned: "There is no secret, that's the secret. There exists simply and unyieldingly the world seen from the outside. For what was called the inside, what was called thought, was only the outside of the world. The painted surface, the sort of crust. The real flesh, the inside of the room, the language and the soul were that reality full of incomprehensible signs, with all its flowers, its leaves, its fruit, its skins, its pebbles, and its footmarks" (22). The world is. All one can do is observe it in order to read the signs it offers and survive. Everything in life should, therefore, be a function of the reading of signs—painting becomes the painting of the body, the better to know it and then to express its life in its context. (The Indians use a stain which is invisible until it has been in contact with the body for a while, so that it seems as though the skin has produced its own design.)

Every action in life expresses a relationship between a man and his world. In the West these actions are disparate. There is no reason for one person to behave like another. There are no stable recognized patterns. Everything is in flux. The Indian is sure of his relationship at any given moment. Hence his actions become rituals. He is not an individual but a manifestation of the life of his tribe and what he is doing reveals the whole society's view of itself. In this context painting, dancing, and singing are expressions of the group's existence and are the means by which life is affirmed: "The Indians do not make representations of life. They have no need to analyse events. On the contrary, they live out the representation of mysteries, they follow the painted marks, they talk, eat, love, and unite with each other according to the indication given by magic. Art, real art for the first time, art and no longer miserable self-interrogation of the individual facing the world. Art, since art is the impression of the universe on the human group and the direct link between each cell and the whole" (43).

Art is there to integrate man into his surroundings. It acts as camouflage, as a defence against the dangers of existence; and, at the same time, it states the position of the human group in the larger movement around it. So it is natural that Indian art should eliminate the concepts of originality and of individuality, which are destined to attract attention. Attention brings overexposure, which is tantamount to speedy death.

The most extraordinary expression of this sense of community of assets is in the description of singing offered in *Haï*. "There exists one single voice: that is the most mysterious thing about Indian singing. When an Indian sings he abandons his own voice and borrows a new, alien voice. . . . Men, women, children sing with the same voice, so that it is impossible to distinguish one from the other" (75–76). Language is deformed beyond recognition, the individual is concealed in the group, and the group disguises its voice: "The musicality of the singing is like a second, parallel language, that cannot be mastered, whose real consequences are unknown and which could well be a way of deciphering it for those who are normally kept at a distance by language" (30). "Indian song . . . is not only a prolongation of language, it is also its defence" (82). The Indian protects himself thus because his voice is his personal property—his soul—which is doubly revealed when he sings. Singing draws attention both to his language and to his (human) nature. He is revealing his position, his kind, his essence. At the same time singing is both a release, a cry of pain, and a mounting of tension which takes him beyond his normal self, his usual relation with his world, and makes him receptive to the *surreal*: "The ultrasonic voice carries him into another universe where language no longer plays the same role, a universe where man neither addresses himself nor other men, where doubts and questioning cease to haunt him. The voice is an instrument of recognition, it goes through the thin screen of mist and draws the outlines of extrahuman obstacles" (83). Through his song (each Indian has his own), the singer traces his identity within his cosmos. But he does not reveal himself and this statement of himself to others. LeClézio tells us that the Indians sit in pairs and sing alternately, quietly into the other's ear. Should one of a pair fall asleep, the other continues alone. The affirmation which is the song exists for itself in its singing. It has no need of decoration, recognition, applause—all of which would indeed be dangerous to the soul which is finding expression in the music.

A way of liberation that has been offered before in LeClézio's work appears in a different form: "Through song, the Indians are perhaps the only ones to have realised the Zen ideal. They practice the uselessness of the temerity of creation, they live it right to the end, that is right to the absence of philosophy and morals. Indian song has no other aim but that of being sung. . . . An Indian knows he will find the only proof there is, the only truth inside himself while he is making way for the alien voice which was in the depths of himself' (86–87).

Singing is liberation through the intense energy it requires and generates. Because of its potency it is always accompanied by alcohol, which eases the way from the outside Indian to the inner voice.

Drugs play a similar role which leads one step farther toward ability to see, to read signs, to hear the voice within. Hence their role in Indian society.

IV *"The Spirit Datura": Résumé*

This fragment describes four occasions on which the author drinks *Iwa*, the juice of datura leaves. The initiation is gradual. The first time Colombie, the Indian, gives him juice which has been cooked nothing happens. The second time LeClézio is given raw juice and after a while has a vision of a magnificent bridge. Then he is afraid and the air around him seems to turn into a gigantic spider's web. The third time he is allowed to roll and squeeze the leaves himself. This time he catches a glimpse of a blue giant on the other side of the river but nothing more. (The dose was less than the previous one.) On the fourth occasion he accompanies Colombie to Colombie's own datura tree and selects his own leaves as well as preparing them. He sees the spirit world, their roads, bridge, and village and is invited to a festival there.

V *Commentary*

Most noticeable in this brief passage is the sense of ritual involved. Certain movements must be made a certain number of times in order to please Iwa, the spirit of the datura so that he will permit the initiate to enter his domain and thus to be able to *see*. Colombie says that he can see into bodies, can see souls and spirits. Most powerful is the author's desire to be accepted by Iwa and his fear that he may not succeed: "I feel that I am very close to the truth, everything will now be decided . . . if I fail: expelled, and cast far away from Iwa, sent back to the darkness of a little man without magic, without adventure, to my darkness of a little reasonable man. . . . I shall only be allowed *my role as actor in my life*, *without ever crossing to the other side. The side where you cease to act in order to become your own audience as well"* (117; my italics). Here we find the theme of masks we have met so many times before, the sense of self-awareness and, of course, by the actions themselves, integration into a stable system which both reveals and protects.

As far as it is possible to tell, some idea of what *In Iwa's Country* might have been can perhaps be gleaned from Carlos Castenada's books. LeClézio states, however, that those are the kind of books he did not wish to write, that Castenada had betrayed his teacher— thus proving that he had not understood what had been shown to him. Such speculation is not fruitful. We can perhaps say that just as *Haï* was made up of *Tahu Sa*, "the all-seeing eye," *Beka*, "the song festival," and *Kakwahaï*, "exorcised body," so the movement of initiation, singing, and exorcism can be used as a description of the relationship between *Haï*, *In Iwa's Country*, and *Mydriasis*. *Haï* shows us the way; *In Iwa's Country* would have been the extending of perception; and *Mydriasis* is an exercise in exorcism in that it is a deliberately reconstructed hallucination. *Mydriasis* is a piece of literature, a constructed vision, which by its very nature returns us to the Western world of scientific possession, of measurement, and self-consciousness.

VI   *Mydriasis*

Mydriasis is a medical term to describe the dilation of the pupil of the eye. This can be caused artificially as one effect of taking certain drugs; and since, in this work, LeClézio refers to *le breuvage* ("the potion")—the term he uses consistantly in "The Spirit Datura" to describe the juice he drank—we may assume that he is describing the visions produced by Iwa.

The movement is very similar to the one described in *Haï* though couched, of course, in different terms. In fact, the themes and images are ones with which we are now familiar: words, solitude, eyes, sun, fear. The book even begins with a reference to concrete, with its implication of the city.

VII   *Eyes*

As its title suggests *Mydriasis* is concerned mainly with eyes and seeing. At first there is total darkness and no reactions "because the eyes, by remaining dim, have extinguished everything in the body"

(10). Everything is black, even the light and the drug: "The eyes no longer know space. They have turned inside their sockets and are looking toward the center of the head . . ." (14).

Next comes intense cold, fear, and meditations on the thoughts of stones. During this time the quality of perception changes: "Sight is a cry which resounds interminably in open space, a cry that no ear can measure. The bitter potion has opened a window in the front of my body and in an instant the soul goes out, spreads out in space, and flees away" (20); the result is a terrifying solitude which gives at the same time intense pleasure. But a new concept of sight takes the visionary beyond fear: "Eyes are no use. They are not made for seeing. When you have learned that, you are no longer afraid of the darkness or the void. Eyes are engines for going in the other direction, toward the future, toward unknown countries, dreams, things of that nature" (22). Everything is swallowed up in the blackness. All words are gone, language is in matter, it disappeared with the setting sun.

Gradually through the blackness forms begin to appear and with them the threat of other eyes—the eyes of the crowd from *The Interrogation, Fever, The Flood*—and the need to use one's own. Danger abounds because, "To see is to let escape the living matter that you have in yourself, that which you received at birth which was inside your mother. Eyes, distended womb through which life will go out" (28). Eyes have become doors which let parts of oneself escape and also let things in. Everything is now light in the vision and the eyes do not change: "They do not close their pupils to filter the violence" (29).

The light comes shining out from inside man and he turns inside to look just before the body disappears and the eyes float free searching for light. They are generating their own energy because of the drug, and they are free of the constraints on perception normally imposed by language: "To see is no longer to have eyes. The screens where the universe switched on and off are broken. Since there is no sun, no moon, no night, there can be no more eyes. . . . That opening will not end. *When the soul has left the body moves about freely among all things*, it will no longer want to return to its old person" (38; my italics). Not only is he now free of language but this now allows him to hear the voices of everything else in the world. All things affirm their existence. His eyes are burned out, and he can no longer maintain any distinction between himself and the universe.

(This is a theme of the early works, including *The Ecstasy of Matter*.): "You can no longer say . . . that there is the inside and the outside. You can no longer pretend to be yourself, to be alone. You will no longer know where the world ends or the soul begins" (42). In the past, words and eyes conspired to keep things out, but this is no longer possible, and the eyes are the hemispheres of the night sky. They offer man the only infinity he can ever know, if he is prepared to liberate them: "You see with the brain directly, directly from the world toward the center of the body" (49). This idea is developed further until it achieves the statement in *Haï* that the secret is that there is no secret. This time it is expressed in terms of vision: "You see: you see nothing because there is nothing to see but only to be" (52). With this awareness he has escaped definitively from the "gaze" of ordinary life where seeing is connected to creation and destruction. His eyes have found their real occupation—looking into himself forever.

Immediately there is a movement outward and he has the feeling of being high above the world, looking down upon it with an eagle's piercing sight: "Nescience is greater than conscience, it opens the face like a fruit and you see, inside the shell, in the flesh, all that jelly and all those seeds: the world" (158).

There are signs everywhere to be read, but it was not until he became blind (in the darkness of the drug) that he could see. He finds himself inside a global consciousness, seeing with others' eyes, inside their thoughts and their language. This vision he thinks he will keep: "The eye will not go out" (61); and it is open to everything. The final vision is one of the Eye of Night inside which we all gather "where the energy of sight is produced" (62). At this the sun rises.

VIII *Darkness*

The major part of the text is concerned with darkness, and the language is such that there seem to be three kinds of darkness superimposed one upon the other. First there is darkness created by the drug. Here LeClézio's descriptions are very similar to the ones given by Henri Michaux in *L'Infini Turbulent (Turbulent Infinity)* (see below Chapter 12). Michaux also experiences utter darkness in similar circumstances, darkness followed by bright light.

The second kind of darkness is that produced by the absence of the sun. This is the darkness of *The Flood* intensified. In fact the following statement taken from *Mydriasis* could well be a comment on the meaning of François Besson's action: "Those who put out their eyes are on the other side of their eyes, they see things undamaged" (39). Besson did not wish to see and so put out his eyes, with the result that he saw much more clearly than before.

The third darkness is the blackness inside the body: the long night before birth. The drug offers a rebirth into a further awareness and as this takes place the original experience is reenacted. The parallel is suggested on several occasions by LeClézio's language and it is emphasized strongly by the illustrations which accompany the text. Drawn with the accuracy of anatomical plates, these are strange distortions of the human body which express birth pangs and trauma in all its violence. From this darkness comes a new light of understanding which would seem to be akin to LeClézio's concept of God as he described it to Pierre Lhoste in 1969: "I think God is infinity, the infinity of psychoanalysis as well as of drugs. It's that sort of opening that every being has in himself that makes him search, move around, write, open doors even if he shuts them again immediately."[2] *Mydriasis* is an attempt to break out of the finite into a wider vision of man and his situation.

IX *Conclusion*

The three texts brought together in this chapter show a remarkable homogeneity. Born of the same culture, expressed through the same awareness, they show a pursuit of the same end: liberation from the self as it is defined and constrained in the Western world.

In an interview with Pierre Lhoste at the time of the publication of *War*, LeClézio was asked what interested him in Panama. He replied:

The possibility of living with the last free men. It's a necessary experience to gain while it can still be had. In Europe we are slaves: we live the lives of slaves in a world of slaves. The Indians in the Panamanian jungle still live freely. They know the things free men know.

Do you think the Indians live happily?

Very obviously. They are people who live without any social hierarchy, in perfect equality, without religion. They are without everything which makes the history and loss of Western society, that is, the fact that some people are more intelligent, richer, more powerful than others. They ignore all that completely. They don't want to know about it. That, for me, is proof of their happiness.[3]

This is a proof that we cannot share unfortunately as we are not exposed to its development in *In Iwa's Country*. A large piece is missing from LeClézio's description of the world.

CHAPTER 10

The Giants

The Giants[1] takes up the theme of *War*, continuing the latter's obsession with supermarkets and department stores. This time, as the title indicates, we find ourselves in a superstore, Hyperpolis, which is an enormous all-embracing shopping mall. It is probably safe to surmise that the description of Hyperpolis is based on an actual shopping mall, Cap 3000, which was opened near Nice shortly before this novel was published and which shares a number of Hyperpolis' salient characteristics: it is beside the sea and at the mouth of a little river. White, surrounded by parking lots, it has in its center a huge, high hallway with an escalator going up on one side, a staircase on the other, a fountain and an information kiosk, around which sprawl and beckon the various commercial outlets.

The giants of the title could well refer to shopping centers such as this, centers whose form and contents are dictated totally by the theories of modern marketing. Within the novel two other interpretations of the title are offered. First, it is suggested that the giants are the "Masters of language" and the "Masters of thought" who control Hyperpolis: "The Masters are speaking. . . . Giants do not speak with words as men do" (G 161). Or alternatively, in a fairy-tale type context, the people are referred to as a sleeping giant who could awaken and overturn the whole city-state of Hyperpolis.

The title is ambiguous—like all effective advertising copy it conceals a number of psychological attractions beneath an obvious message. The tone is set for the whole novel, but before we study it further let us look at the "story" with which we are concerned.

I *Résumé*

Bogo the Mute sits on the parking lot at Hyperpolis or on the beach nearby and watches the world. Vast crowds go in and out of the store and are hypnotized by the colors, sounds, forms of the things around them and move as in a trance, without any thought of their own. Tranquilité fights this mindlessness as she walks through Hyperpolis to meet her friend at the information desk. The colors affect her. Later her friend drives to meet Tranquilité (Tranquillity) and this time she is confused by the letters and words along the road. These two girls have a friend, Machines, who pushes trolleys in Hyperpolis and who is fascinated by mechanical objects. His favorite place is a Gulf gas station. He walks along the road to it every day, even though he is afraid of the cars roaring alongside him, because in the gas station he is at peace. Nothing is hidden between the words and their obvious meaning there. It is a haven.

Meanwhile Bogo has left home and is dodging the police in Hyperpolis. Next we see Tranquilité and Machines lying on the bed in Machines' room. They are afraid of being overheard and of the mirror so they write notes to each other; Machines writes that if Tranquilité will not go away with him he will burn Hyperpolis. Finally they break the mirror: it was a two-way mirror. They see another room behind it and three men run away.

As a result of this, Tranquilité is questioned while attached to a lie detector. The security men want to know who intends to destroy the shopping complex. At the end of the session the interrogator turns up the piped music heard continually in the store and under it she hears "Hyperpolis must be burned."

Bogo is on the beach watching seagulls when two girls go by, row out to sea, and commit suicide.

Interspersed between these events are perorations on language and thought control, pages of pseudoadvertising copy, and quotations from various sources—mostly ancient.

II *Structure*

Hence we see that the text of the novel has three levels parallel with those of the title, and these levels are directed to produce three forms of understanding through the intellect, the imagination, and the subconscious. All the levels give the same message: we are being controlled more and more by mechanical and psychological means for commercial ends. Our individuality, autonomy, and freedom of thought are at stake. We must react.

This tripartite form is typical of LeClézio's writing, but this novel, unlike the preceding ones, has little time for introspection. The narrator (I) is busy explaining the state of affairs today, lecturing the reader about his situation rather than turning in on his own impotence. In support of the outwardly directed didacticism LeClézio's writing is terser, less lyrical, and more direct in its movement. The cosmic writing is there still, but it is clear to read and has no hint of mysticism. *The Giants* affronts a crisis. Philosophy is for more peaceful times.

The novel has a very loose construction in which the different themes are intermingled in no definite order. There are sections concerning Bogo the Mute, Tranquilité and her friends, and the state of the enemy, and these alternate more or less, though there is a predominance of explanation in the middle of the book. Right at the beginning and right at the end Bogo watches Tranquilité and her friend walk across the beach. This gives the impression of a circular movement which has been completed, but this structure is not stressed elsewhere. The whole text is enclosed within pages of commercial copy and interspersed with advertising slogans, ciphers, language, etc. The overall impression is one of a gradual infiltration of an alien tongue. In this way the structure and visual impact of the book reinforce the story it unfolds. One is tempted to use yet again that much overworked phrase "the medium is the message."

III   *First person narrative*

The first person narrator addresses himself directly to the reader in the opening lines of the text and continues to do so unequivocally throughout the nine sections left to him. (Bogo has seven and turns up in the last one, as do Tranquilité and her friends.) He opens and closes the novel and has a function rather like that of a general briefing his men. He calls us to action: "Man has become a subject of study for man, the only subject of study. Free yourselves! Stop being studied! Nothing has the right to know man. Because, in order to know, one must be above" (*G* 18). Then he denounces the enemy, the men who are masters of the modern world, the commercial magnates and the psychologists in their employ: "Some men use all the science, all the intelligence, all the power in the world in dominating the others. . . . They have full power over colors, smells, tastes, and distastes . . . there has never been so much power, so much warfare . . . there has never been so much money. The forces of beauty and desire cut through the masses . . ." (*G* 30). These men control and sell everything. They create and control also our desire to buy certain things by adjusting our concept of the life we should lead. "Alien words have entered my brain," writes the narrator, "I should like to be something other than an echo" (*G* 30). This is the basis of the struggle laid out in *The Giants*. It is a struggle to avoid living in a prepacked life in a prearranged décor repeating secondhand thoughts in slogans and clichés.

It is possible that the cry to arms has come too late; but the narrator believes that thought does exist in all matter and can be mobilized to protect us against the enemy. The enemy are the Masters of language (*G* 127–33) who have contaminated our words and with them invented fear, anguish, a new *mal de siècle* for man, who now finds himself an alien in a world other men have built. The Masters' language is explained to us with examples (*G* 161–75). It is fast, powerful, and designed to command. It is insidious and very clever: "The Masters' language takes no notice of the hatred it brings into being; or rather, it measures, judges, and despises it. Each time it invents a new desire, the Masters' language has invented hatred of itself at the same time. It has set it up in the center, in the middle of its act like a necessary negation of it. Hatred is the illusion of liberty and the Masters' language distills the word *liberty*" (*G* 170). Within its control is included the feeling of reacting against control.

Next the narrator explains the power of electricity in the Masters' plan (see below p. 129) and, having shown the source of energy, moves on to the inevitable conclusion: the appearance of the Masters of thought. Their activities are presented satirically under the title of Varioum Broadcasting Properties. The powers the company is given are extensive, and its properties are clearly the minds of us all: ". . . In the dream it makes men dream, the Masters' thought has laid the most terrible of its traps. Men and women see each other, and their own gaze, as it turns back toward them, puts them to sleep and devours them. . . . Consciousness is like a strong room that the sleepers construct around themselves and which walls them in. . . . Do they know that the Masters were spying on them in the very center of their consciousness, that they filmed them all the time in their ridiculous kingdom of solitude?" (*G* 244). Having described all these dangers the narrator hopes that his indications will bear fruit and that an authentic desire for liberation will grow until man manages to free his words and use them himself for himself once more.

This is the lesson given throughout *The Giants*. The theme is laid out clearly at the intellectual level and is presented twice more throughout the novel, once by the fictitious characters and once in the pages of advertisements, which have been devised and constructed as carefully as any of the plans against which we have been warned.

IV Plot and Characters

At the imaginary level we are offered a rudimentary plot of the really old-fashioned villain and hero kind. This is the first plot we have found in LeClézio's writings, hence its role in the novel is of some interest. It unfolds very slowly under the watchful eyes of Bogo the Mute. First he observes two girls who walk along the beach and go rowing. This scene at the beginning of *The Giants* has an exact parallel at the end except that on the second occasion the girls die. These two would seem to be Tranquilité and her friend, if we consider the answers Tranquilité gives to her interrogator, and are the heroines of the story. We learn that they are afraid of and struggle against the hypnotic effects of Hyperpolis (Supercity), to the extent of trying to think and managing to write poems. Tranquilité, in particular, is aware of the traps around her wherever she goes. She is always on the watch for hidden microphones and cameras. The girls have a friend who works as a shopping-cart collector and his name is Machines. He is the hero of our tale because he tries to burn Hyperpolis after Tranquilité has refused to go away with him.

We know very little about these three except that they seem simple and gentle and dislike being bombarded by slogans and messages at all times. We have a brief description of their appearance (always supposing that Tranquilité and her friend are the girls on the beach), but they are not developed in any way. They are merely ciphers, names to be manipulated at will. Their major attribute is their fear, which distinguishes them from other people in that they react to their surroundings. They are afraid, panic-stricken, paranoid in the face of an unknown enemy—whoever it is who runs Hyperpolis, the faceless Masters. The fear is proven justified when Machines breaks his mirror and there are three men behind it, when Tranquilité is taken away by Hague of Hague System Inc. and cross-examined, and yet again when the mirror in Hague's office lights up to reveal five observers who give orders.

There are eyes and ears everywhere. There are the unknown ones in Hyperpolis and there are the police of whom Bogo is so afraid and whom he recognizes everywhere:

There were policemen of all kinds: grey, green, black, and blue ones. There were some along the sides of the road in a sort of phosphorescent red jacket. They were pretending to dig holes in the tarmac. . . . But their eyes were slit at the edges for they were always secretly watching . . . there were some who looked like anybody else . . . there were some who were pretending to light a cigarette with a metal lighter in front of the cinema door. They were looking at the stills in the windows. But Bogo the Mute knew that their gaze rebounded off the window and went spying behind them. You had to be careful. . . ." (G 229)

Machines is taken by the police for trying to burn the shopping mall, and the ultimate irony is that he was taught by the building itself that that was what he was to do. Presumably Machines is the most susceptible to the message because he is the one who spends the most time in the building, and he is simple, straightforward. He has no resistance to the sophistication of subliminal conditioning such as is practiced in Hyperpolis. The message is revealed to Tranquilité:

Now the young slave perceives something else. Behind the music, a very soft murmur, a whisper similar to the humming of bees.
". . . you understand what it is. . . . It's the Hyperpolis experiment. . . ."
She perceives every word. It is a single murmured sentence repeating without stopping behind the soft music:
HYPERPOLIS MUST BE BURNED
HYPERPOLIS MUST BE BURNED. . . . (G 285–86)

The reason Tranquilité has been referred to as a slave is now clear. Everything she does is conditioned. Even Machines' apparent revolt was organized by the "Masters." Hence the suicide at the end. The girls see no other escape.

We are in the realm of nightmare; or rather, and here the reason for the simplistic plot becomes clear, we are watching a horror comic, one of those in which the helpless hero and heroine are tossed about utterly at the mercy of some all-powerful faceless master and his minions. The scenes we are given in *The Giants* are very easily transferable to the medium of the comic strip because they are very visual. The three principal ones, Machines' room, Tranquilité's Kafkaesque questioning, and Machines' setting fire to the building, are etched in our minds with great precision, for LeClézio is a master of descriptive writing. The Gulf station, the girls in the boat, and Tranquilité's walk to meet her friend are equally transferable to a series of pictures. This is black humor; LeClézio is using modern techniques to wage his war on modern society. His characters are helpless. They have no mind to analyse, and they decide on no actions to carry out. The only medium which can express their plight and make us realize the horror of it is that of the comic to which we are accustomed. Hence, for example, the tone of Bogo's description of the policemen.

Bogo the Mute thus comes into his own as the artist's symbol for himself sitting in the corner of each drawing watching what goes on, seeing it all but rarely involved in the action. He is an alter ego who can help us to understand. Indeed, in good LeClézio tradition Bogo provides us with an analogy of the whole situation in his observation of the sea-gulls around him on the beach: "The hyena gulls don't like men. . . . On their long legs the hyenas prowled slowly around the white gulls and they searched out a bird which was too old or too young, a bird that would not defend itself. They were interested not in the pieces of bread, but in the birds. That was the kind of thing to be learned on this beach" (G 293).

Bogo is in the position of Adam Pollo. He has managed to stay outside society for the moment, but surely this cannot last. Either the police will get him, or else he imagined the chase and thus will probably go mad in his turn. He is the symbol of escape from the modern world, but his life on the beach does not offer a viable alternative to life within society except as total exile. His role in the novel lies rather in his rejection of language. This action is both a sign of revolt and a safeguard against Hyperpolis and its like. He finds the uses to which language is put either stupid or dangerous and wishes to avoid both. In the early scenes he goes to Hyperpolis to listen to conversations; and his doing so enables LeClézio to ridicule normal superficial exchanges while engaging in some visual humor at the expense of language:

Bogo the Mute heard more or less this:
"ffiKult koRS chiLDren, you know, and theeenn, as for all the Rest"
"Uhhuh"

"See, but in the INside that we DOEnt see, Nthing SIMilar exiSTs. Nothing similar."
"YeeSS I THiiin kijunderstand" (*G* 75)

Because of his activities Bogo understands language; and therefore when he chooses to employ words he exploits their full potential. At the end of the novel, like a fairy godmother, he will release this power and destroy the enemy:

> But one day language will come out of the camps, and will break down doors, windows and walls. . . .
> No one can be called Bogo the Mute any longer, when that moment comes. The little boy who can talk. . . .
> He says: "La la luz . . ." and immediately all the light bulbs burst.
> He says: "Autorat," "Autorat". . . and immediately the black roads are covered with big black rodents. . . .
> Looking at this other man is enough . . . the little boy looks at him, and slowly he pronounces the Master's name,
> "OEUFS!"[2]
> and immediately his face becomes as flat as a photograph of a stranger.
> Those are the things one can do when one has learned to speak. (*G* 306–8)

The use of language is important because it is a means to express and control thought, a way of communication at all levels. *The Giants* is, indeed, a highly skilful example of multilevel writing.

The story we are offered is in no way realistic in its presentation. It is in the manner of a parable or a fairy tale, and the names of the characters prepare us for this kind of didactic fiction. Machines and Tranquilité are reminiscent in their form of Buttons and Cinderella, and their relationship is somewhat similar. Bogo the Mute sounds like the name of a dwarf or clown. Here we are perhaps being taught another lesson. Fairy tales have at least two levels of message which they transmit to generations of children. On the surface is the conventional victory of good over evil, while beneath this is a much more realistic description of the violence, traps, and dangers of existence. Our tale also has two levels, the first being that we must fight against evils that undermine our human essence and attributes. The second is that we are being conditioned into the decisions we take. This level is, of course, obvious because LeClézio blows open his own construction by revealing to Tranquilité the

methods used in Hyperpolis. We are therefore made aware of the
practice of subliminal conditioning and can watch for it elsewhere
(in comics for instance!). The problem lies in the end of that
explanatory sequence when the man behind the mirror says: "The
experiment stops here. . . ." This was an *experiment*, and the next
time we see Tranquilité she is killing herself and her friend. Was she
conditioned to die also? Just how far does this go? LeClézio has told
us that language is *piégé* ("full of traps"): "Traps have been laid for
the colors, noises, music, forms! Traps have been laid for the light!
Traps have been laid for desires," he writes. In which case, how far
is his own work free of traps?

The answer to such a question is negative. While LeClézio is
explaining our situation to us on the intellectual level, illustrating it
with characters and plot, he is giving us an object lesson in the pages
of advertising copy.

V *Advertising Copy and Other Experiments*

The Giants opens and closes with several pages of advertising
copy which many readers have no doubt turned unthinkingly and in
doing so have missed the lessons LeClézio is giving there—though
they may well have picked up the command "Hyperpolis must be
burned" which is set in tiny type in the bottom righthand corner of
every page of this kind. These pages contain not only regular copy
but extracts of reports on studies done for advertisers, reports on
psychological tests which can be used to increase the efficiency of
advertising, and other forms of thought control. They reveal to an
alarming degree the power and attitude of those he calls the
Masters—only this time the words are not LeClézio's and the quotations are not fictitious. People are doing this in our world today;
doing it *to us*. Let us look at some of the passages cited. The novel
opens with the following statement printed at the top of the page:
"The ultimate success of biocontrol could be man's self-direction.
The directed subjects would never be authorized to think as indi-
viduals. Several months after birth a surgeon would equip each
child with a socket in the scalp with electrodes penetrating chosen
zones of cervical tissue. Sense perception and muscular activity
could be modified." At the bottom the final line of the same report
ends as follows: "or completely controlled by signals from state-
owned broadcasting stations." This is *Brave New World* and *1984*

combined, and it is coming into being around us despite all the warnings we have had. LeClézio was right to quote the prophets in *War* and refer to Apollo's oracles in earlier works; he is the latest in a line of Cassandras who have all been ignored. "Minds can be shaped to want your products" we read; yet what kind of people are being created?

Buick: "Gives you the feeling of being the man you are."
Jean Patou: "the most expensive perfume in the world." (G 235)
Kolynos, "the toothpaste of the *Stars.*" (G 132)

Among all the typographical extravaganzas that we know so well are interspersed the explanations given by the creators:

    Cheskin: candies
inferior category: bright red metal container+blue
                  ribbon: 50 cents
superior category: pink cardboard container+magenta
                  ribbon: 9 cents
Instinct for survival (weapons, food, houses)
        for domination (possession)
        sexual (jewelry, clothes) (G 88)

In order to deal with the sexual revolution Fleischmann's Gin asked for Louis Cheskin's advice. He suggested a slight alteration in the label design that the average buyer will not even notice but which will increase the company's sales considerably. The label was rectangular: Louis Cheskin had the corners rounded which made it more feminine. (G 132)

Human reactions and basic instincts are being manipulated at will for commercial purposes: "Ernest Ditcher: 'One of the main tasks of publicity in the conflict between pleasure and guilt is not so much to sell a product as to give permission to feel pleasure without feeling guilty' " (G 132):

Suggestion of docility.
Automatic suggestion.
Automatic imitation (G 324)

There we have the sequence of development, a sequence which has been spelled out on the first page of the last block of pseudocopy.

VI *Diesel Power*

While miraculous progress has been made in the technical domain, *the science of the human machine has been lamentably neglected.* This is the science of shaping and adapting the behavior of industrial personnel. Thanks to this, the skill and knowledge of a workman will be equalled by his capacity to show cooperation with regard to his work, his boss, and his fellow workers. We really see *man made to order* here, ready to give himself totally to the building up of a great industrial future. (*G* 323 my italics)

This is the danger we are being warned about in *The Giants:* the total annihilation of the individual. Fear of such destruction is the reason the real title of the book is a sign that everyone in Europe knows and reacts to instantly. ⚡ = Danger of death (by electricity usually). LeClézio is teaching us the language of our enemy, showing us how our own language can be undermined, warning us against subliminal attack. He even offers a basic bibliography for any reader who wishes to learn more on the subject and, for those who have not understood his teaching, he practices subliminal conditioning of sorts—a counter message runs through the novel. The names of the enemy are listed, of course. The variety of letters and words is displayed consistently. We find pages of bad typing, pages of language distorted by typography, repetition, computer printout, and finally several pages of Algol 60, the language of machines, the one the computer understands. We may tend to disregard them all, but in one way or another, consciously or unconsciously, we are affected by them. We are in the same situation as Tranquilité's friend, surrounded by signs, afraid, and unable to escape: "The letters were numerous, more numerous than bats in a cave. There were so many letters that you could no longer see the sky, the ground, houses, or faces" (*G* 86).

One way of escape is through thought based in culture—in the basic values of the human race as expressed in language used properly for the edification of man rather than exploited for his abasement. And this force is mobilized by LeClézio throughout *The Giants.* He tells us of his intention in the opening pages:

I SHALL NOT INVENT NEW ACRONYMS
RATHER I SHALL TRY
TO BREAK THE OLD SEALS

Then he offers Chinese symbols for birth and death, another for heart and ear (G 133), references to several Eastern religions, and a Celtic battlecry: SLUAGH-GHAIRM. He writes at the end of the book: "There are a lot of things to say or do with words. Fear, death exist when the words are outside, when they try to get in or conquer. But when the words are inside, the Masters of language suddenly become small and their ruses ridiculous" (G 130). We must regain control of our language and thought. Literature is a source of power in such a war.

VII *Electricity*

As we have seen already the title of *The Giants* is really a lightning bolt threatening death, and electricity is the power by which the masters achieve their aims. It illuminates their neon signs, runs their lie detectors, computers, and as a last resort the electric chair. The first time we encounter electricity in *The Giants* the whole of the novel is foreseen in one image by Bogo: ". . . light hits the macadamed ground and the roof of Hyperpolis, and the metallic sheet of the sea and each surface sends back the burning rays along the ground, rather as if there were millions of electric sparks making a cloth. Or as if everything had been sprayed with benzine and suddenly someone had thrown a match. A heat explosion going off horizontally with one big flat flame" (G 36–37). Next we meet electric women who murmur in Tranquilité's head (G 60), followed by the electrically powered words and letters that frighten her friend (G 92). Another element of brainwashing is frequently constant light making rest impossible, and this also has its place in Hyperpolis.

There is no place to hide. The gaze of the indecent light comes to find you wherever you may be. Perhaps, when it gets dark. . . . But it is never night-time. The giant turbines that are not known send electrical current along the lines. All the time from one tower to another, over the valleys, mountains and roads and the electricity spreads through Hyperpolis, reddens all the little wires at the same instant, all the helium, carbon, and neon tubes, lights up the air molecules, the mirrors, the polystyrene balls, lights up the women's bodies, the men's bodies, and that is why there is no rest. All those electric light bulbs which are inside men and women would have to be turned off, but it is impossible, the turbines do not stop working, electricity does not stop running along the cables between the giant pylons." (G 111–12)

In this extensive quotation the two aspects of the title are brought together. The giants bring the danger, for electricity can get inside everyone; it makes menacing noises in their houses and watches everyone all the time through wall sockets. It can betray man to man, as we have seen in the episode concerning the lie-detector, and *in extremis* it can kill; but it can also be overcome. When Tranquilité tears the wires from her body and dashes toward the plug her torment is over (*G* 286). Bogo also works against the power—by transmitting against it on one occasion and by trying to destroy it on another. There is a chapter devoted to a boy's fight against the power of electricity—but ironically his story has been recorded on tape—hence the evidence is preserved by electricity. Before this there has been another chapter in which the narrator talks to us directly about its uses and power.

Electricity holds the world in thrall, and man is captive because his world is imprisoned in a vast spider's web of cables which separate the earth from the sky. Liberation means freedom from this power which enables certain men to manipulate others. It is the silent, faceless enemy and master behind the men in grey suits who watch and give orders against which *The Giants* is a battle cry. The first pages of copy flaunt

ELECTRA OF BALSAN, ENRAGED DOMINATORS
self-cleaning maxi-oven, instant burners with pilot light programmer, electric plate with tester
[YOU] WHO WANT TO BEND THE WORLD

Balsan is close enough to Belsen for the concentration camp image to be established in the readers' subconscious. In reaction come the first lines of the text proper, "I am telling you: free yourself! It is time. . . ." The text closes with a repeat of the imagery: "The Masters want to drink blood. They have a horrible need of men's blood to live what they live. . . . When will this end? Speak! Shout, speak, or be mute but do not let the Masters' language do whatever it likes!" (*G* 315).

The penultimate lines are ambiguous. Is the electricity weak because man has brought in a force from space, or it weak because the masters have turned it down and man can do and perceive nothing? Can we or our world be switched off? The final lines suggest that there may be an escape on the other side of fear, "If there is another side, to be free" (G 320). The idea of liberty is coupled with doubt, and in the last advertising copy the concentration camp image returns yet again to haunt us with the Goebbels Experiment and the remark, "I look at this sign and I'm afraid." The sign is "The Lightning Sign," in which the title, the sign, realizes at last its third and final meaning: that of Hitler's secret police. The dreaded S.S. wore the lightning flash as their insignia.

The comic strip satire has dissolved into the nightmare of total, brutal domination. All humor has gone from the first and final message, which is directed at both our conscious and subconscious perception. The need to fight for human thought and language is a matter of the survival of the race. No wonder the girl is no longer called Tranquilité at the end of *The Giants*. Tranquilité is dead.

CHAPTER 11

Journeys to the Other Side

Journeys to the Other Side[1] offers the ultimate escape, one to which all of LeClézio's work has been leading, and it is difficult to imagine where he may go next. (At the time of writing no other book has yet been published.) The end of *The Giants* prepares the reader quite specifically for this text. In *The Giants* we read: "Perhaps it was better not to talk too much about all that. Perhaps it was better to talk about dreams. . . . But it is possible to go to the other side of one's fears, if there is another side, in order to be free" (G 230); and the text ends: "One must write, think, and act enigmas." Some of these enigmas are resolved by the appearance of *Journeys to the Other Side*. By the power of dream, language is taking the revenge promised in *The Giants*, and is taking it in the very form threatened: "Words like the cobra's [naja's] fangs, which will stand up and go into the flesh, and their speech will be their poison [the words of the Masters]" (*The Giants*, G 306); for Naja is the ringleader in this escape from the commercialized city life previously described, the heroine of this masterpiece of evocative writing. *Journeys to the Other Side* is a reverie from which a multitude of dreams begin. One is reminded of an old text quoted byAndré Breton and Michel Butor entitled *Dreams and Ways to Direct Them* and a second mentioned by Butor, entitled *How to Achieve Happiness through Dreams*.[2] *Journeys to the Other Side* is an incitement to flight by daydream.

I *Résumé*

The novel begins with a description of the beginning of time when all was under water and closes with a parallel description of the end when all will be stone. Between these two we follow the travels of NajaNaja and her friends, Gin Fizz, Sursum Corda, Alligator Barks, Louise, Leon, and Yamaha into the heart of objects and elements and experiences provided by the everyday world: an olive tree, smoke, rain, fire, a bat, along reflections on water to the setting sun, and so on. NajaNaja is an expert in such excursions out of herself and her friends are learning the way of liberation. At other times NajaNaja tells stories. Finally she disappears and leaves them to manage for themselves.

II *Flight*

Again the main theme of the novel is one of escape from the city and its pressures; but this time the means are very simple, means that are at everyone's disposal—those of the imagination. *Journeys to the Other Side* are a series of daydreams beginning in ordinary things around us and pushed as far as it is possible to develop the sense data at hand. This is not fantasy per se but deliberate examination of things we all see and usually pass by. LeClézio has the faculty of putting himself inside things and describing them in their life as if he were the things themselves. We have all watched a cat or an ant or a bat, all sat at the foot of a tree, or watched the sun set over the water. All we have to do to take part in *Journeys to the Other Side* is to watch the world more closely and allow it to lead us on. LeClézio builds castles of silence, palaces in the clouds and in the fire with a seductive pen.

The reveries are mostly elemental (we are reminded constantly of Gaston Bachelard's books *Water and Dreams*, *The Psychoanalysis of Fire*, etc). LeClézio sees people as particles within a material system, and with regard to *Journeys to the Other Side* he comments: "What I can say is that the relationships between men are not very interesting if they are not subordinated to that real astral and terrestrial presence, if their communications are not made at the same time through the elements, if their words are not in the flames, the rhythms of the earth, the cycles of water and wind as well."[3] This link with the universe is now offered as a means of escape. In previous novels LeClézio's characters have walked and walked around Nice, have traveled around the world to find a spot in which they can be at peace; the solution of daydreams then seems a very simple one. Surprisingly, however, the narrator of *Journeys to the Other Side* writes that they also are looking for a country which they need never leave. Although they can travel for a while into each marvellous country no dream will last forever, and from time to time they must return from their journey.

The problem of flight is not solved yet, though "the other side" provides the best alternative so far.

III *Giants*

Journeys to the Other Side is sprinkled with references to giants which remind us of the previous text, and *The Giants* prepares the way for *Journeys to the Other Side* in a way we can only recognize in retrospect. Toward the end of *The Giants* everything exists in superabundance and is about to explode. The explanation given is this:

Perhaps it is so because the giant is about to wake up. Perhaps . . . or perhaps it is only a spasm in his deep sleep. . . . How can we know who the giant is? . . .

But they are not really desires which swell up and make their threatening noise. Perhaps it is simpler than desires, something terrible and beautiful in life that we do not stop. It is something which does not need words in order to appear, something as vast as the sea, as hard as shingle, as cold as the sky, as hot as the sun . . . this force, this passion belongs to nobody. They are real and tangible, they are alive. What should we call this force? . . . You must transform it into a cold pebble and hide it deep inside yourself. You must give it its real name, ONYX. . . . Then you stare at the stone and the black light which springs out of it burns you to the depths of your innards. . . . The pitiless gaze scrutinizes everybody, it goes through walls, masks, clothes and armor. It is a metal needle that can pierce all secrets, go to the end of all distances. . . .

I should like to say FREE YOURSELVES like that, with a voice like the gaze of the onyx, a voice that does not hesitate. The flight of seagulls, the air, the sun, the wind, the trees, the waves, the pebbles and even the white domed buildings say the same thing. But before saying it you must see it and hear it, you must know it." (*The Giants*, G 302–5)

We have quoted at length because in this passage we find an abstraction of the appearance, powers, and fuction of NajaNaja. She has black hair and eyes and dresses in black. She can see through anything at any distance, she is the force which gives the desire to be free and which teaches how to understand the messages of everything in the world.

The way to NajaNaja is via the sleeping giant, and we meet him again from the other side in a dream. NajaNaja steps into a man's dream and travels with him *past* the sleeping giant to the top of a cliff from which the man dives into the sea. He has escaped from civilization into infinity. NajaNaja was tempted to waken the giant but does not because she is warned about his temper. He does not look ferocious—but we have already learned in *The Giants* that appearances are deceptive.

The next giant in *Journeys to the Other Side* establishes the relationship of the one novel with the other again. NajaNaja is traveling among the stars when she comes face to face with Bételgeuse, the giant. This one too is dangerous because of its inherent attractiveness: "Bételgeuse is so big and so gentle that it is difficult to leave. You must go backward again, planing in the void, closing your eyes so that you no longer see the star that fills you like a thought, the vastest thought in the universe" (G 214). This is the atmosphere and effect of Hyperpolis and the feeling is confirmed when almost immediately afterward NajaNaja is drawn irresistibly toward another star: "NajaNaja looks at the star and feels a funny hypnotic sleep come over her. It is Algol, the demon . . . he flashes on and off all the time and throws his evil messages out through space . . . the uncertain white star draws you into his field, paralyzes your will, quashes your desires . . ." (G 215). Algol 60 is the name of the computer language cited in *The Giants* and used by the Masters to produce just such an effect as that described. To escape, NajaNaja must jump into the river of the Milky Way and be carried toward stars with names which come from the beginnings of human culture: Scorpion, Hydra, Wolf.

This image of a giant is ambiguous. There were three interpretations offered in *The Giants*, and here the recurrence does little to clarify its use. Early in *Journeys to the Other Side* NajaNaja imagines people as big as boats who sail through the town like huge machines. Others stand still like buildings and little people live in them: "The truth is that they sleep on their feet. Their sleep lasts for months, years, centuries even. Perhaps they will wake up one day and start a long march toward the sea" (G 85). These are sleeping giants who fit into one of the levels of *The Giants* without any trouble. The problem is that NajaNaja describes herself as a giant in whom the others live (G 276–79). The difference would seem to be that she is not asleep, for she is already beside the sea, and to her the sea is not made of stone as it is when seen through the eyes of the previous giants. Perhaps it is safe to suggest that any giant is a symbol of a Master. Sleeping giants are man-made worlds who imprison us, giants who are awake are living worlds. NajaNaja envisions one stage further: "Perhaps we [the giants] are in the mouth of another giant, bigger still, sitting on the white rocks of his teeth and watching his large blue moving tongue coming and going in the light" (G 279). We are left to wonder whether he is awake or asleep.

IV *NajaNaja*

Presented as a giant NajaNaja is the all-embracing mother goddess who has been an important force in Western culture from time immemorial. She appears to her friends in their sleep, after a series of festivals, dances, and sacrifices to Mexican gods and speaks to them thus: "I am very big, I am immense. You can no longer see me now because you are no longer outside me, you are inside my body. I am the one in whom you live. . . . I bear the mark of eternity on my brow" (G 276). She describes their world as her body within which they live and from which they can be expulsed. The birth images that exist in *The Flood* and *Mydriasis* are here in a different form. NajaNaja provides a protection equivalent to that of going back to the womb. One element of her speech is ominous, however. She says: "It's as though you were in a department store and it is inside me" (G 276). This comparison refers us to the ambiguity of the figure of the giant. Is NajaNaja as dangerous in her elusiveness, her mystery, and her power as the Masters of the commercial world? Is the way she offers as confining as the other? If we look at NajaNaja in her other forms, we can perhaps find some kind of answer to this nagging question.

V *Elf*

NajaNaja is both very big and very small. The essence of the character is her constant metamorphosis: "She changes her name, she changes her person. One day she is there, another day she is absent, so absent that no one could find her. . . . But it is difficult to talk to NajaNaja beginning at the beginning because she has neither beginning nor end" (G 25). She is magic. She can become a cat or a bat, travel to the sun or walk along the sun's rays on the water. She can become invisible and walk along with people helping them or playing tricks that surprise them. NajaNaja has all the secrets necessary to penetrate all things: "She won't say anything, she will not open her mouth. But in walking along, and we run after her until we are puffing like seals, she shows us the way to every country. She doesn't look back to see if we are following her. She walks along with a regular, elastic step . . ." (G 33). The image is that of the Pied Piper of Hamlyn who also showed the way to new and marvellous countries. NajaNaja seems to step from a storybook. She is the perfect companion for any imaginative child who has grown up a little and come back for her friends—a Peter Pan for adults.

Her friends are learning the art of traveling to the countries she offers, and during the course of their experiences improve a great deal. They have already shed reality to a certain extent and achieved a certain mobility through their names: Gin Fizz, Alligator Barks, Sursum Corda, Yamaha, and finally Louise and Léon, who operate like Siamese twins even to the extent of sharing their dreams. These names reject ordinary contact and, more important, they are not fixed. In the body of the text there is a chapter of names NajaNaja gives to them from time to time; and as the novel proceeds Yamaha becomes Camoa while two others are changed into Teclavé and Palmito. On another occasion, in a bar, they all take on the names of their drinks.

This mobility of name gives a mobility of essence. Throughout his work LeClézio has shown that knowledge of a name gives a basic understanding of the object in question. Now we find people who have escaped the constraints of stability. "If you are somebody—and I don't wish it on you—you are the same size every day" (G 25), writes the narrator. Further, "If you are somebody, and if your name doesn't change, you have swallowed your face. . . . Yet people had an absolute desire to be somebody. They said they were building their lives, that they represented them, that they were at last going to do something with their lives" (G 24–25). These people leave scars on the world where they have passed, and at the same time they wear themselves out. Rather than wanting to know, they should experience the world as NajaNaja and her friends are doing. NajaNaja has achieved the ultimate aim. NajaNaja is nobody—in the sense that she can free herself of her body at will (or rather, perhaps, that she can take on a body at will).

NajaNaja teaches her friends to enter into objects—to pretend, for example, that each is an olive tree, but to pretend with such intensity that they become trees. Then they become migrating birds, the wind, and go into the fire with NajaNaja. When they have enough expertise to find their own roads to other countries she takes them on a journey along a long road with a shining white city at the end of it. To get there they all walk for a long time: "NajaNaja walks in front. If she crossed the sea to go to the other side we would go in too" (G 272), we are told, and when they arrive in the city they are no longer in Nice (rue Shakespeare, etc.) but in Mexico for religious festivals, dances, and celebrations. (This sudden shift happens also at the end of *The Giants.*)

At this point other aspects of NajaNaja are revealed. She ceases to be the elvish young girl and becomes first a snake and then the giant we have discussed above.

VI *Snake*

"It's as though there were snakes sliding along the ground. NajaNaja stops in the square and begins to dance. We dance with her . . ." (G 274).

NajaNaja is the name of the Indian cobra, the most fearsome of the cobra family, a snake which is considered sacred. It is the one most frequently used by snake charmers, and thus the importance of dancing in NajaNaja's life takes on another significance.

The link with India can be developed further perhaps if we think in terms of the snake as a symbol of chthonic transcendence, bringing messages from the depths of the earth (and hence, by analogy, from the collective unconscious); for from India comes the symbol of the entwined serpents on a staff which we are familiar with in its Greek form as a symbol of medicine and healing even today. These are called the Naga serpents. Their very name and the fact that there are two snakes suggests a connection with the double name of Naja-Naja.

Early in the book NajaNaja is introduced in terms of a snake:

NajaNaja deserves her name. Supple, slim, and long, she slips between the stones, the plants, the people coldly and without any effort. . . . When she walks in the streets of the town she is not really there. She is traveling in her own country, a country of salamanders and snakes. . . . Snakes are never where you expect them to be. They are somewhere else. NajaNaja slides along, disappears into open doors, and then comes back out through secret holes. Her country is full of hollows, dens which have at least two ways out. (G 42–43)

Snakes shed their skin as NajaNaja sheds her roles. They love the sun and light. Snakes hypnotize their prey. Naja's friends will follow her wherever she goes even when they are terrified, as in Mexico when they realize the full implication of an understanding of the universe—man is sacrificed.

The snake is the symbol of Egypt and of Mexico, two sun oriented cultures. The snake is solitary, and we are told that NajaNaja does not like to be disturbed. She appears when she chooses and her friends accept her isolation. In an interview with Claude Mourthe already quoted, LeClézio combines the two elements:

> Without wanting to play on words I think there is a correspondence between the word "solitary" [*solitaire*] and the word "solar" [*solaire*]. I think that continually living in, passing through, or thinking about these solar countries which are governed by this single presence of the sun . . . where the first thing that matters in life is the discovery, when you are very young, of that double, the black shadow attached to your feet . . . in countries where the sky is enormous the light is enormous, it is natural that you should be struck by the isolation and that you should only really feel yourself each time you find yourself facing the sun and that you should therefore associate all thought, all reflection with that confrontation. . . . This solitude, this exposure to the sun are inevitable . . . these moments with the sun, with yourself and your shadow that is, cannot be shared.[4]

Into the combination sun and self enters a third element, shadow, and with this shadow comes the whole weight of darkness, night, and, if we may return a moment to Peter Pan and his shadow, loss of innocence. Hence the snake is the natural Christian symbol also, and NajaNaja becomes the amalgamation of Eve and the serpent.

At this point NajaNaja takes her place among the other women of LeClézio's novels. No longer an eccentric girl in the style of Giraudoux's lighter-than-human heroines, she takes on full force as the summation of all women: young girl, tempting, innocent, and untouchable, sexual power responsible for all man's faults, goddess who enfolds, protects, and rejects. NajaNaja is everywhere, charming, perfidious, and, above all, fearsome.

LeClézio has operated the displacement which created mother goddesses in the first place, only this time NajaNaja is born of his own creation. Roch Estève metamorphoses into a woman, J. F. Paoli walks and walks to find or forget one. Joseph Charon sees Maria Vanoni as the explanation of death *(Fever)* and Chancelade has a vision of NajaNaja in *Terra Amata* (eight years before the publication of *Journeys to the Other Side):*

For a few seconds everything in the world becomes woman. . . . He [Chancelade] entered the leaves of women trees, women grasses, women algae. . . . The light trembled in the air like gossamer hair. The strange silent figure danced inside every flame, and in the deepest hollows of the seabed slept the wide-hipped grey silhouette . . . he . . . became a woman, the same invincible woman who possessed the earth from the dazzling center of her body, and who was no more either thought or word, but simply a sign of life eternally deployed throughout the universe.[5]

Here is NajaNaja in all her metamorphoses, even to that of Watasenia, the underwater creature from the beginning of time, which is also the period before birth.

To show the danger of the snake in *Journeys to the Other Side*, the metaphor is transferred from NajaNaja herself to the whirlwind: "It is a sliding, twisting knot, or else the body of a large, cold, magic snake casting its coils around him" (G 183–84); and it is transferred to Harmattan the sandstorm, who will be instrumental in creating the stone world of Pachacamac where in the last moments of metamorphosis ten vipers appear:

Slowly, slowly, they went up the flight of steps. The dreams were abolished because they came to the end of their story. On the huge platform, illuminated by moonlight, the snakes moved toward each other. The labyrinthian paths led to the sand platform where the vipers slithered about. There was no noise, no speech, no thought. Then the snakes joined themselves in a knot, and the earth, space, sun, and even the moon swimming in its waters, were no more than circular regions, today: the ten-headed serpent was in the center. (G 308)

The atmosphere of this last paragraph is reminiscent of another text of LeClézio's in which snakes predominate—*The Snake Garden*. The text begins: "on the road of sleep," wording which might indicate that it was originally to be included in *Journeys to the Other Side*. In it the sleeper is walking through a silent garden. He is afraid and cannot understand why until suddenly he sees that the garden is full of snakes—among them:

        "NajaNaja
     on its back is the sign of the serpent
  A monocled cobra which bears a death's head"

and this piece of writing ends with the statement "We are the snakes."[6]

The metaphor of the snake links NajaNaja to Harmattan and thus to the final section of *Journeys to the Other Side;* her image as a woman is linked closely to her hair which is long and flowing and is mentioned on numerous occasions. By this hair she is connected to another force of nature which speaks for itself in the text: Light Rain, who is the absolute opposite of the sandstorm except in so far as both are all-pervasive and both cut off the light of the sun.

Light Rain offers comfort and gentleness, the feeling of being lighter than air. You get to her palace by means of her hair, an image which reminds us of Rapunzel in her palace, and also recalls the description given by Chancelade of "gossamer hair" or rather "spider's-webby hair," with all the implications of imprisonment. Hers is the realm of water and peace which links NajaNaja with the first section of the novel, with Watasenia and its tentacles which flow like hair in the water.

Light Rain achieves her effects some of the time by telling stories, stories with no beginning, no middle, and no end, which nonetheless have the power of entering the body of the listener. In this way and others she hypnotizes her captives until "One is nothing more at all, one has no more desires nor memories" (G 161), a state which is reminiscent of the effect of Hyperpolis on Tranquilité and of NajaNaja's stories on her friends. NajaNaja remains awake however, thus sharing another characteristic of the snake: its lidless eyes which, by giving it an ever-watchful gaze, are responsible for its traditional attribute of wisdom.

The character's links with the whirlwind, rain, and Pachacamac, Mexico are made explicit early in *Journeys to the Other Side* when LeClézio writes: "NajaNaja is a bit like the plumed serpent" (G 52); for the Plumed Serpent is Quetzalcoatl, god of the wind, life, morning, and the planet Venus. Venus was thought to have long hair because of the planet's fiery trail, and hence a connection is made with Harmattan and Light Rain as well as the idea of love which NajaNaja certainly inspires. The clearest link, however, lies in the the story of the god rather than in his attributes, for he moves successively under the earth, on the earth, and in the heavens. Hence the parallel between Quetzalcoatl and NajaNaja is very striking.

The connection with the Mexican deities reaffirms the danger-ousness of NajaNaja, however, as well as her power. The threat to man is clearly stated: "Finally we want to climb up to Tonatiuh Ixco in order never to lose sight of the sun. But we must cross unsure areas . . . avoid the regions of tlalloliniliztli, the water serpent, the snake Xical, Chimalcohuatl, the water coyote, the water hare, the tzoniztac, she who stands up like a woman, and when the sun is covered by cloud, the tzitzimi, devourers of men" (G 275). NajaNaja joins the serpent women who have caused men's downfall, through the ages, by the dreams they produce. Quetzalcoatl rides across the sea on a raft of snakes in order to achieve rebirth. For the West also the snake has long been a symbol of transcendency and renewal because of the way it sheds its skin. For this reason also it is a symbol of eternity especially when depicted as Ourobouros, the alchemical circle made by a snake with its tail in its mouth. As alchemy and snakes are linked and as the aim of alchemy is the symbolic recreation of the universe—that is, alchemical experi-ments attempt to reproduce a series of transformations leading to perfection (gold), which at the spiritual level symbolize rebirth in the world before the Fall of Man—then we see that the use of the snake metaphor for NajaNaja is one which explains the numerous journeys into which she initiates her friends. She is helping them to reexperience their world in its original purity as it was before man dimmed his own sight by imposing a restricted amount of self-acquired knowledge between himself and his environment.

Here the true ambiguity of the snake symbol becomes apparent: the Serpent (the Devil) tempted man to blunt his own perceptions and bring death into the world (the cobra [NajaNaja] is a symbol of death), yet the snake by its very makeup is a symbol of wisdom and renewal. Does NajaNaja face an eternity of teaching, of being mis-understood by those who listen, and of watching man fail to regain paradise again and again? The idea is taken further in her third role.

VII *Storyteller*

NajaNaja's third role is, therefore, that of storyteller. It is in-teresting to note that in the interview quoted above LeClézio con-tinues directly from the contrast of sun and shadow to the talk of writing: "Also the novel and the act of writing in general are not of the day but of the night. Under the lamp which represents a fallen, controllable sun . . . to retransmit a little of that energy, reflect it attenuated, confused by words. . . . Like those fires which are lit when night falls and which help men see each other from one side of a valley to the other."[7]

This concept of warmth and light transmitted by stories is one which appears directly in the novel: "You do not listen to NajaNaja's stories to remember them, you listen to them to hear her voice and feel warm" (*G* 232). The extraordinary thing about NajaNaja's stories is that they are intended to put her friends to sleep. First she draws them in very close to her by speaking quietly and then sets them dreaming by her fantasy. As they learn from her they are able gradually to create their own stories, first taking up where she left off and then managing for themselves. Like her they learn to listen to the stories the rest of the matter of the universe has to tell so that they can journey into other realms: "Now it's up to us to tell the stories, not to kill time nor to make noise but to go to the other side of everything" (*G* 291).

NajaNaja is a reciprocal Scheherezade. Each is the total woman who can hold a man in a thousand and one ways because she knows all the secrets of the earth. It is their situation which is reversed. Scheherezade tells stories to prolong her own life, NajaNaja tells them to preserve her friends who cannot cope with life at all without their necessary dose of stories. Scheherezade's tales are her protection against death whereas NajaNaja seems to lead her friends toward it. The most enticing journey is the one to the far horizon, and that one cannot be accomplished in life.

NajaNaja is the ultimate weaver of spells, the woman who can transform a man's life so that he walks with her through unknown countries, to the end of the world. The image is a double one: the reveries are those she offers and those she is. All her metamorphoses are sexual, those of snake and hair most obviously so. She is a dream of the unattainable female, multiple, desirable, for whom the search goes on forever.

Adam Pollo's frantic search for Michèle does not differ significantly from Alligator Barks,' Yamaha's, and Sursum Corda's quest for NajaNaja. In both cases the man is unable to make contact with the woman. NajaNaja is described in terms of magic while Michèle has human attributes; but throughout the works of LeClézio the problem is the same. As the narrator of *Journeys to the Other Side* puts it with regard to Sursum Corda's attitude, "It makes for misunderstanding."

VIII   *Narrative*

In *Journeys to the Other Side* LeClézio has returned to his earlier habit of writing a cosmic preface and epilogue to the main body of his text. This time he has created an aquatic world inhabited by Watasenia, a brilliant member of the squid family who is the underwater power equivalent to NajaNaja in the period before the formation of land, or in its personal interpretation, the time before birth. Human life is just one of the Watasenia's many dreams.

The last section shows the end of the world when all has turned to stone and only snakes remain. It bears the title Pachacamac, which is the name of a very old city in Peru, a city dedicated to Viracocha, the Inca god of rain. One of the sons of the Sun, he was thought to be the creator of the world and human sacrifices were made to him. By the title then a link is created with NajaNaja in the form of Light Rain and with the religious festivals described, as well as with the snake form itself. The bare rock is the most extreme solar landscape imaginable, that to which the sandstorm aspires. Hence the central section is connected to the frame by the stories of the two elemental forces who are allowed to speak for themselves. Only *Light Rain*, *Harmattan*, and *Far Horizon* do this and by doing so establish themselves as facets of NajaNaja: gentleness, power, and inaccessibility.

The book is written in such a way as to create reverie in the reader. It has very little forward momentum, each section being one journey, one dream which is fully developed, or a series of enticing flashes of potential. In each case the reader is tempted to stop reading and dream on for himself. *Journeys to the Other Side* is constructed to have the same effect as NajaNaja's stories which are interspersed between the dream trips.

In order to change the tone and tempo there are sections which deal with NajaNaja's friends traveling in their car for example—some of the journeys are therefore real and realistic—but such excursions are always resolved by a dream or a story. There are also short quotations of an enigmatic sort which appear here and there throughout the book. These vary from:

I have finally understood
I hear a song
I see a flower
Oh, may they never fade (G 57)

to "The mouse dreams dreams that would terrify a cat" (*G* 163) and
"Do you hear the murmur of the torrent in the mountain? That is
where the entrance is" (*G* 309) and seem to be invitations to create
one's own journeys to the other side.

The text is recounted by one of NajaNaja's friends, who remains
nameless and who speaks directly to the reader most of the time.
The tone is familiar (he varies from *tu* to *on*), easy, and gives the
impression that the reader is listening to information and to stories.
By this means NajaNaja is put at a distance from the reader, separated from him by the narrator, who himself takes on an aura of
magic because he tells things he should not know if he is an ordinary
member of the group of friends described. The atmosphere and
style is that of a fairy tale, and *Journeys to the Other Side* demands
total suspension of disbelief. LeClézio is trying to open our eyes as
widely as those of a child, to put words into the things around us as a
child does, to help us recreate the wonder we had in the world
around us and which we have lost. Inevitably this gives a certain
innocence to his language and a poetic energy also. LeClézio has
always shown himself to be a master of description of the sort known
as set pieces—the storm in *The Flood* is a superb example— but
here there are moments when he surpasses his own best writing as
he captures the beauty of reflections on the water or transmits the
speed of a bat. He says that ". . . writing seems to me to be the
possibility (the faculty) of making whatever is dumb speak. That is to
put language where it should not normally be . . ." and continues:

. . . I am quite sure that we all have that possibility, that luck of sharing
with the universe in the first years of our lives, and then we lose it. But it
isn't far away. It is hidden in the words of our language and is likely to
appear at any moment, and we shall hear echoes of the words of trees,
rocks, water, air, and flies. It is hidden in our gaze, and we are going to see
eyes opening on every side. It is inside our bodies, and we shall be able to
feel all those movements, all those vibrations, all those pulsations that are
all round us on all sides.
It is enough to be in silence, don't you agree?[8]

With these words LeClézio takes upon himself the role of narrator. His book is an attempt to open both eyes and ears, to exploit
language until it gives up its secrets. The character he has created
within it is a personification of the power of imagination and an
embodiment of the forces of healing, transcendency, and rebirth.

She offers a new life, a cure for the ills of the world we live in and against which LeClézio and his characters have been struggling throughout this study. We are invited to follow NajaNaja as far as we can by the transformation of our own reality. This is a book to dream with.

CHAPTER 12

Influences

THE question of influence of other people on an author is always a thorny one to be handled with great caution. Given the
restrictions of this volume we intend to discuss only the writers on
whom LeClézio has published studies himself. Basing ourselves
exclusively on this material we can then say with certainty that the
points offered are those which LeClézio recognized in the other
author, whether or not he made the transfer to his own work. The
people in question are Henri Michaux, Isidore Ducasse, Comte de
Lautréamont, and Antonin Artaud. In the case of all three writers
the similarities between their work as presented by LeClézio and
LeClézio's own writing are many and striking. Whether their books
influenced LeClézio's writing so that he came to resemble them,
whether he chose them for study because he identified with them,
or whether his criticism distorts their work because he sees only his
own preoccupations in others, are questions too great to be dealt
with in one chapter. Therefore, we shall offer the reader the comparisons which emerge from the texts available at the moment
(1975) and leave him to use the material as he sees fit.

I Henri Michaux

The study of Michaux, "*The Problem of Solitude in the Works of
Henri Michaux,*" is by far the most developed of the three, running
some one hundred and twenty-four pages of typescript.[1] It is the
earliest (finished in 1964), so a knowledge of Michaux dates from
before the writing of all LeClézio's *oeuvre* except *The Interrogation*
and may be considered contemporary with this, the first novel.
Reading the dissertation in the knowledge of LeClézio's themes,
style, and preoccupations is an extraordinary experience, for it occupies more and more the position of a book of prophesy. One could

147

almost say that LeClézio is analysed under the pseudonym of Michaux.

Michaux's major themes are given as the problems of solitude and communication through language, each of which have two opposing aspects. Hence the artist is being pulled in two directions at all times. The opening paragraphs of LeClézio's dissertation which purport to be an introduction to Michaux's attitude are seen, in retrospect, to be a statement of LeClézio's understanding of his own position:

> Today in a world given over to multiplicity, the indefinite, outflow, a sort of immanent and yet already imperfect apocalypse, it seems as regards truth that there is no longer room for anything but an immense and fanatical solitude. This isolation, which is realized slowly, constitutes the fundamental theme of our time. Man, deprived of unity, offbalance, dispossessed of his very self, finds himself as he was in the beginning: prey to terrors, marked by anguish, having a presentiment of dangers and chasms he cannot understand. He seeks out brothers to attenuate the fear within him by sharing it. But he can find only enemies.
>
> Man's attitude is double: while on the one hand, having become aware of his isolation and fragmentation, he gives in to the dangerous sickness, he lets himself go almost wantonly, on the other hand, in the grip of an unspeakable anguish he searches desperately for fixed points to hang on to, faces, human voices which remind him of who he is and why. (1)

Thus there is a movement toward rejection of the world and a simultaneous need for contact with it, both of which are born of a clash between the artist and his context. The artist lives in an unresolved love-hate relationship with everything around him which causes him to vacillate between aggression and self-protection, between anguish, doubt, suffering, and a state of revolt and vengeance. Such a movement is both a cause and a result of his solitude, and at the same time expresses his attempt to gain some hold both on the world and on his own being—again the movement is a double one. LeClézio describes it thus:

> Indeed, Michaux belongs totally and uncompromisingly to the world of the living. He would not know how to be alien to it, and it is by virtue of this attachment to the common struggle that he is subject to this ambiguity, this cycle which is alternately active and passive. . . . In the period called "withdrawal" we first notice an attack; the poet attacks to live and his aggression has many forms; it can be anger, cruelty, rage, anguish, humor,

irony, desire, hatred, or love; next we see a period of asceticism; the poet discovers the reasons for his struggle inside himself.

In the period of isolation, of "passive" solitude . . . we shall see first of all what is fleeing from Michaux, what evades his power, what really creates his isolated state. Deprivation, then annihilation. . . . The deprivation will be everything the outside world refuses the poet, every means by which it condemns and destroys him. Annihilation will be the inevitable result of this condemnation: introverted, Michaux watches the substance of his own existence dissolve and fade away.

This dialectic of solitude would be incomplete, however, if there had not been a search, throughout the writer's life, for conciliation, for a way out. (6).

And this conciliation perforce consists in part in the maintenance of the poet's sense of self.

The struggle creates a language in which it can express itself in all its diverse aspects: a language which can serve as a protection or as a weapon, a language to express hatred, rage, fear, and suffering, a language for the two facets of destruction, that of the self and that of the outside world. It is forged by a combination of humor and cynicism together with what LeClézio calls "descriptive vocal gestures" (45); these are syllables with onomatopoeic sense only. Hence Michaux sets up a system of defence and counterattack which, as we have seen already, LeClézio uses also. His work moves much the same way as Michaux's. Like Michaux he is afraid of the world, apart from it and yet of it. Like Michaux, he needs to understand himself and his surroundings and his work has the same poles as those he sees in Michaux's writing. Again his statement refers to both writers:

This quest for an ideal language is both desperate and brotherly: as easy social structures crumble, as the imprisonment walls thicken and the chasm of the being dissociated from himself deepens, the cry of rage and desire becomes more powerful, more exact, more in tune. The poet seems to forge his own surest weapon against isolation: becoming used to his blindness he has been able to develop other senses and feeling his way has shown him, if not the ways out, at least the layout of the labyrinth where he has been abandoned. (2)

This search is accomplished through language and also through the poet's life. The nonaggressive phase of Michaux's exploration expresses itself in flight of various kinds, and here we find ourselves at the heart of one of LeClézio's major themes. First there is physical flight to India and to Brazil, and it seems that India has on Michaux an impact similar to that of the Central American Indians and indeed the Asians (of *The Book of Flights* and *Haï*) on LeClézio. LeClézio, quoting Bréchon on Michaux and Michaux himself, writes: "For Michaux, India was the first great way out of isolation, 'the first people who, *en bloc*, seem to respond to the essential, who look for satiation in the essential, a people finally who deserve to be distinguished from the others.' (Bréchon, p. 21) For Michaux, to come out of his matrix, to love almost, demands total freedom; what he asks of human beings is 'decency' (Michaux, *Barbar in Asia*, p. 65). A certain nobility also, an 'interior life'; what moves him in Bengal is people's 'detachment,' that closed and tranquil aspect which characterizes women and old people" (28).[2]

The problem for Michaux is that he is always obliged to return from his journey.

For Michaux travelling is fleeing: a real flight far from the greyness and boredom of Europe; it is a reflex which is essentially childish in so far as the taste for adventure that "gives one the feeling of being on unfamiliar ground" is a puerile one. But, knowing that, Michaux is "a hunted traveler so to speak." The travel theme is an extremely important one in Michaux's work: we said above that adventure was a way for the poet to break out of his "sphere"—indeed Michaux's personal struggle is the one he arranges between his sensitivity and his intelligence. An extremely concrete struggle whose issue can only be rending and hatred, a struggle which is like the one faith could have with lucidity. (94–95)

Flight from the society he knows is one means of respite then for Michaux from the war which LeClézio sees to permeate the first part of the poet's work, then comes a second stage, that of exploration which is both physical and psychological and which is pursued through drugs:

If we begin from a chronological point of view we see that this "itinerary" of Henri Michaux is marked by two major stages: war, drugs. . . . A first period from 1923 to 1943 where the poet's research seems to focus around themes of revolt, cruelty, and suffering. After the "test" of the war, a second period takes shape . . . psychological and parapsychological themes, analysis of the human being taken to the limits of what is possible. In 1956 first experience of mescalin which will provoke Michaux's third major "itinerary": to achieve knowledge of man through what is most inhuman in him. (91)

Here again we find the essential themes and means used by LeClézio: war and flight used in a desperate struggle for self-discovery and expression. Drugs are just another phase of exploration, a way of gaining a freedom and experience similar to that offered by travel yet on another plane. (Here Michaux is linked to Artaud and the net of influence draws tighter.) LeClézio writes:

. . . with Antonin Artaud drugs cease to be considered as "pleasure material," they become synonymous with revelation, they are a means of exploration. So you understand what an extraordinary means of truth and communication hallucination can represent for a solitary, withdrawn man like Michaux; drugs are weapons of the solitary and despairing; as Artaud wrote, with them "man is alone, desperately sawing away at the music of his skeleton, fatherless, motherless, without family, love, god, or society. . . . And the skeleton is not made of bone but of skin, like a walking dermis. And you walk from the equinox to the solstice, fastening up your own humanity yourself." We are a long way from a pleasure drug. . . . (113)

Drugs offer an exploration and a withdrawal simultaneously. In this context, recalling LeClézio's birth trauma images in *Mydriasis*, we note a remark to this end he makes about Michaux: "One would willingly say about this 'badly situated' poet . . . that he has one foot in this world, one foot in the other which is essentially intrauterine" (38). He then draws the following conclusions:

The "inverted" universe of the poet is "the universe of before man's invasion", the original experience of before "consciousness." (from A. Hoog, *Poetry and Psychoanalysis*, Net. 1946, p. 122) But this experience cannot be anything other than a violent one. Michaux suffers from a "void," he feels "accursed" in flight. Then withdrawal looks like a painful, despairing act; it is a struggle against being overrun by the world, against invasion by the others in himself. . . . This fear of being possessed by others is deep in the work of Henri Michaux. . . . In order to flee, Michaux must "withdraw," extract himself from the world, and fight himself after a fashion. . . . The poet emerges bruised (38–39)

This struggle passes through many stages that LeClézio seems to share: hatred of self and others, exploration of matter, frustration at his own weakness, dissociation of personality, metamorphosis, meditation in which he finds what LeClézio calls "thoughts for participation in Being" (98) rather than thoughts for thinking; to arrive finally at the stage LeClézio has reached also in *Journeys to the Other Side*, that of the creation of a new world through the imagination. LeClézio's analysis of Michaux once again fits his own work very closely—and yet the dissertation was written by 1964 and *Journeys to the Other Side* did not appear until 1975—first LeClézio quotes Bréchon (94) in his commentary on *My Properties:* ". . . Unable to maintain himself in the world and to possess anything, he aspires to grasp at least a truth. . . . Now that truth . . . exists and imposes itself even upon him with all the evidence of fate. He has chosen to settle in and to exploit by the use of imagination, that undeniable part of himself, which is at the same time the prison of his me." LeClézio continues thus:

. . . the outside world is mystery, pain, and complication; one would not know how to approach it simply in everyday language: no, to remain master, not to succumb, "it is enough to be chosen, to have kept the consciousness of living in a world of enigmas to which it is best to reply in enigmas also." (Michaux, *Passages*, p. 180) Imagination is Michaux's response but [and LeClézio continues to quote Bréchon] "the working role of Michaux's imagination is complex. It is primarily a means of evasion, a more efficient equivalent of travel; it is also an instrument of defence against reality. It is a means of completing creation: it turns man into a demiurge. And it is a means of investigating the universe." (95–96)

LeClézio further comments: "The world of Henri Michaux's imagination is a *useful* one. . . . The poet becomes *seer*" (95). He returns to Bréchon (99): "Imagination is here a magic procedure to change life; not being able to act on 'real world as we say,' the mind works on representation and remodels it to its liking, as do the characters in the *Constructor's Drama*, making a town with a die or being recognised as God the Father." (We have given the quotation in its entirety as this recognition of the artist—or his creation—in the role of God is one we have had cause to discuss with regard to LeClézio himself.) LeClézio's final comment expresses his own attitude illustrated by later works: "This imagination, in fact, is the absolute opposite of egoism: it is not a peace, it is not an ease, a rest—on the contrary it is an awakening, a departure, an *action*—" (96).

The description LeClézio gives of Michaux's work reveals a structure which applies to his own in a fashion all the more striking because LeClézio's work had not as yet come into being. The movement produces the following pattern where alternating moods produce dialectics of response:

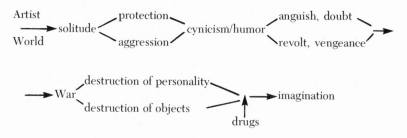

An alternative résumé can be found in the body of the dissertation. It reads: "If you visit Henri Michaux's work what do you find? A terribly rich, complex universe 'where you pass without warning from the most cutting humor to the most rending naked lyricism; from utterly gratuitous fantasy to the most brutal realism; from the description of imaginary countries to that of very real ones (and you don't know which are the most real); from a metaphysical tone to that of interior monologue and from maxims to epic poetry.' "[3]

Given that this covers LeClézio's writing also it is interesting to look at the explanation he offers: "This very richness is what creates his isolation: Henri Michaux is an introvert almost in the clinical sense of the term; the universe has got inside him, turned into chaos, and can only get out with pain and difficulty; that outside nakedness that characterizes Michaux is the lack of means of communication; the excess of internal richness results in a human poverty in the poet. He has no natural movement toward other people because he feels the impossibility of coming out of himself" (34–35). It would seem that the younger man recognized his own problem in the older one and consciously or unconsciously followed the latter's path toward a fecund creative release for both of them through an assumption of mankind into an almost mystic use of the imagination.

For both the need for linguistic expression is imperative, and this links them both with Lautréamont. Michaux states that if he had not read *The Songs of Maldoror* he would never have dared to be a poet. LeClézio claims their need is a biological necessity and justifies it thus: " 'Writing' is the normal reaction of a living being, alone, who must continually prospect, accomplish, consume what surrounds him. And who is led by a double attitude of withdrawal and unfolding to destory what he discovers" (5).

Henri Michaux is linked to Lautréamont and Artaud by LeClézio—first to the adolescent poet by the physical need to formulate a violent expression of his pain—this at the beginning of his life as an author, and at the end of it, his association with Artaud's belief in drugs as a means to reveal man's condition, again expressed as pain. It is not, therefore, surprising to find LeClézio studying Lautréamont and Artaud on his own account. Given his apparent identification with Michaux's progress such would, indeed, seem an inevitable development.

II *Lautréamont*

After finishing his master's thesis on Henri Michaux, LeClézio registered to do a doctorate on Lautréamont. This second thesis has never been written (Lautréamont's work did not lend itself to the study of word frequencies LeClézio proposed), but three texts have been published to date: "Poetries to come," a long review which appeared in *Les Cahiers du Chemin;*[4] "The Other is Lautréamont" in *Lautréamont;*[5] and a preface to the *Oeuvres complètes.*[6] Through these we can see what attracted LeClézio to Isidore Ducasse: "More than a book, more than a literary work (because it is precisely the only completed literary work), the songs are a secret, a whirlwind of words born in the depths of man and which must never leave his body, a magic language where the questions and replies interlock, a whorl movement which never stops going from the circumference toward the center."[7]

For LeClézio, Lautréamont has a similar impact to that of ancient mystic thinkers and resembles above all the mode of expression of the Central American Indians such as those described in *Haï.* He makes the point in *Les Cahiers du Chemin:* "The Songs have no age, the mystery of their origin is contained in the very words, in the images, in the breath and their function is not to distract or teach but that: to SING";[8] and it already is a major theme of his preface written some years earlier (1967). Just as the Indians distort their human voice in order to sing and through singing move into a new mode of perception which puts them into closer contact with the world in which they live, so is it with Lautréamont. In the preface LeClézio wrote "A masterpiece of egocentric expression . . . one meaning going toward communication, toward the sharing of language; the other meaning being, directed at the very guts of the one who conceived it, turning back so to speak toward the silent nothingness, origin of its creation."[9] Later he developed this thought: "The truth is that Lautréamont invents his own knowledge here by parodying, deforming, plagiarizing the verbal universe that surrounds him. The great forces of Maldoror do not come from the subconscious (with all the limitations this word has) but clearly, from consciousness, which is not an individual faculty, but a relationship with all human, animal, and cosmic powers. Complexes, obsessions are merely manifestations of this real, organic consciousness whose stage sets are human myths."[10]

Lautréamont has been able to push the exploration of the self to the utmost limits of language, to the point where the consciousness of self has been transformed into "immense gaze vibrating within itself" and a state of abstraction similar to death in *The Songs of Maldoror*. In the *Songs* the author hovers on the edge of madness, caused by total absorption into himself. In the *Poetry* the language changes and the ultimate singular metamorphoses into the universal. Lautréamont explored his suffering to the utmost and in doing so destroyed his initial solitude and with it his egocentricity and personal relation to the world. LeClézio sees in this shift a salvation which he himself pursues in his own writing and which he expresses most clearly in *Haï*, a work which is indeed contemporary with the Lautréamont studies. He writes: "This anonymous art, untouched by the vanity of individual ambitions, this religious art to which Ducasse aspires, is the only one capable of saving man because it tears him away from sterile contemplation of himself and restores him to the community."[11]

Lautréamont uses language to discover and describe "this seething of elementary life." His explosion shakes language out of its rut, dislocates its habitual forms, and frees it. His work is: "The symbol of rebellion against the established order, of the cry against the language-prison."[12] Beyond that "He can speak for all men once more, not to affront them or to seduce them, but to teach them truth and life."[13] And this is what LeClézio is trying to do as well. He, too, is in search of a language which is not the personal property of one man but which expresses universal truths, the movement of the world in its reality—a language which has the communal creativity of the Indian's singing when voices are indistinguishable one from the other as each person joins a communal expression and defense which is also an affirmation of his position in the universe.

This aim LeClézio and Lautréamont share. Many creatures and images can be found also in both authors; eyes and sea creatures are the first to come to mind, but as there is no proof that LeClézio was influenced by Lautréamont in such a choice, we will leave such discussion, considering it beyond the scope of this chapter. The feeling of identification does seem to come through strongly however. In the last paragraph of the preface to Lautréamont's work, LeClézio could have been writing autobiographically, so close is the link between the preoccupations of his criticism and his own writing of that period.

Lautréamont is the center of his verbal property and he does not cease reigning there as absolute master, giving us in every incomplete word, in every trembling sentence, in every cry, the secret of that enjoyment and that great misfortune: absolute solitude. And often the humiliating hope that this adventure in the country of words was dedicated to a sort of death comes as well: when the sentences, betraying their creator once and for all, breaking their old lethargic twitch, slowly unroll their whorls and bound toward us, we who know to make them our slaves."

With his ambiguous closing sentence: "Snakes always keep their venom,"[14] we are reminded yet again of the imagery both authors share.

III *Artaud*

Until now LeClézio has published only one article on Antonin Artaud and this appeared in *Les Cahiers du Chemin*,[15] under the title "The bewitched one." He has, however, said that he is considering a further, longer study because of his interest in Artaud. Already in the material at hand we find a number of points of contact between Artaud and LeClézio, points which in some cases we have already seen in Lautréamont and Michaux. Indeed, LeClézio links Artaud with Lautréamont through the passion of their work and their sacrifice of their life to it. Both works are on the outer edges of what is normally considered literature, primitive outcries from the heart of someone alienated from society, rejecting its values, seeing the world in a different way. And LeClézio values this kind of writing which attempts to tear the mask from writing itself and force words to reveal what is in the world rather than veil it. "Everything happens as though the use of words should invent that other provisionally unutterable reality which was hidden behind language," (57) writes LeClézio. "No life has ever been as deliberately consecrated to life, in *literature* and in the *arts* we see no other example of such a concentration of force." (57) Writing is a way to understand and to survive. "Language, literature, theater, theory are one and the same thing, and Antonin Artaud does not struggle against them as he uses them . . . he struggles with them so as not to die." (56)

The material he uses for his work is himself, so that the whole body of writing is a search for identity through the destruction of various elements of his own sensation. It is a gradual dispossession in search of self, a liberation in the mode of Zen or the Indians (as we have seen above in LeClézio's books) which has a similar result. Artaud sees the individual in a context of which he is no longer afraid after having visited the Indians himself: "There is this collection of forces which are the world, with all its visible and invisible links, all its knots of passion and desire, its vibrations of enjoyment and suffering, and of which the individual is only a small fragment." (61–62) Once he has realized this, LeClézio suggests, the personal element of identity joins the cosmic one of destiny and Artaud has achieved his potential. His power is revealed as *magic*, which he can accept. Artaud thus breaks loose of Western structures and moves into a *yin-yang* swing of creation and destruction in which he makes contact with the essential forces of the world which are too powerful to be sustained by humankind. Once destroyed he works his way back to reestablish the annihilating contact. (LeClézio compares it to an electric current—we see the link with his own work.)

LeClézio attributes to Artaud relations with writing and the world which are very like his own. Thus it comes as little surprise to encounter two steps of the development of the relationship which we have encountered before: those of flight and rage. "Constantly restrained rage . . ." he writes. "He [Artaud] knows . . . he has need of other men, their gaze, their anticipation. He also knows that even in love he cannot expect any understanding except pity or lies. . . ." (58) This is LeClézio's own reaction and that which we have seen in Henri Michaux. The rage is that of a solitary individual, who is isolated from others and haunted by their presence. It is from this feeling of being apart from others and of being watched by them that the eyes and the gaze, take their power both as expression of embarassment and fear, and also of rage and hatred. It is the gaze of him who looks and of him who is looked at on both the animal and the cosmic level.

From this expression comes the movement of escape and the concept of flight which pervade LeClézio's books. Here it is attributed to Artaud: "He has guessed and accepted fright, and flight, the reflexes of a wild animal who suffers, before he falls prostrate, not in order to save himself from his ills . . . but because he wanted to be the master of his own suffering" (61) and earlier, "All is danger, everything is a trap . . . writing is the only means by which Artaud can provide a handhold" (59) then: "He names his ills because they reveal the secret forces by which he is inhabited." (61) Flight is one stage on the way to liberation, the liberation which Artaud sought also in drugs, in travel, and finally—very like Adam Pollo—in madness.

IV *Conclusion*

As we have seen, there are between the three authors who interest LeClézio and himself a surprising number of points of coincidence. All know the civilizations of Latin America as well as that of Europe, and in this context all have experimented with drugs to obtain liberation from the strictures of a Western outlook. They are all solitary figures who seem to be ill at ease in society, and for each writing is an outlet which enables him to express his feeling for his situation, his fellows, his relationship with the whole expanse between life and death.

None of them fit into regular, accepted literary categories. The writing of each one is extremely personal, a poignant cry from an individual intensely aware of his weakness and his anguish, who reacts with violence, pouring his whole life force into the one channel of expression by which he may perhaps contact other people while obtaining some lessening of pressure on himself. Simultaneously, it is a wrenching apart of the social logic of language in order to tear away the linguistic masks which hide reality under comfortable hypocrisy—the hypocrisy the writers cannot accept and which is in some measure responsible for their initial alienation.

They are authors who reject conventions and categories to delve into the recesses of themselves and the world in order to seek a truth, an equilibrium between birth and death. They are the primal scream of French literature, and it is in the force of their relation to language that they come closest to each other.

CHAPTER 13

Conclusion

IN the course of our discussion of individual texts it has become abundantly clear that LeClézio's writings to date function as a cohesive whole. There are constant reflections, echos, and even direct references from book to book as well as within each volume, and successive works take up themes that have already been treated in order to develop them further or offer an alternative statement. A schema of the relationships between the books looks something like this:

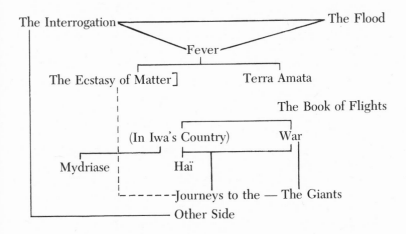

We see that the works tend to go in pairs. *The Interrogation* and *The Flood* offer the poles of heat and cold, light and darkness while telling the same story of bewilderment, refusal, and flight from society by symbolic annihilation of man's faculties of comprehension. *The Ecstasy of Matter* and *Terra Amata* are the theory and practice of human life in Western Europe and hence complement each other totally. The attitudes and preoccupations of the first three novels come together in *The Book of Flights*, with its tale of repeated turning away, whereas the contrast between village and city established in this book provides the division and parallel which have marked the pairs since 1969. *War* shows the struggle against modern city life; and its parallel was to have been found in *In Iwa's Country*—the story of life with the Panamanian Indians. Similarly, *The Giants* has its partner in *Journeys to the Other Side* in which the overwhelming accumulation of consumer goods is exchanged for the seething possibilities of the natural world. And in both the mind leaves the ordinary thinking plane. In the first case under the influence of the subliminal messages broadcast in Hyperpolis the movement is induced by others. In the second case NajaNaja teaches her friends to control their own minds in such a way that they can escape the restrictions of reality for a more universal plane whenever they wish. Simultaneously, *Journeys to the Other Side* provides the missing complement to *The Book of Flights*. The latter showed physical and geographical flight while the former explores mental and cosmic escape through the power of the imagination—a solution used tentatively at the beginning of LeClézio's career in *The Interrogation* and *The Ecstasy of Matter*.

I   Major Forces

Throughout the work the protagonists are dominated by two major influences: the sun and the sea—or occasionally water in some other form. The sun brings understanding, an understanding of things which are sometimes too painful to withstand; thus man tries to escape what the light forces him to see. But everything is focused on the sun; for LeClézio all man's thought and hence the structures he establishes are created around it, for it is the source of revelation. It is reality. At the end of one of their conversations, P. Lhoste asks LeClézio what he judges to be really essential in life. LeClézio replies:

The sun. There is no doubt of it. An ascertainment you make at birth and which becomes more precise throughout life until death is the presence of the sun, the organization around the sun. There is nothing that is not connected to the sun, even religions, even philosophies, even societies. When you have the good fortune to live in countries where the sun is present most of the year, you have a better chance of understanding things that come from society, things that come from education but that solitary, burning presence that returns every day, that you never stop seeing, is the only reality.[1]

The sun is therefore the archetypal Apollonian force of intelligence.

The complementary influence is water, and it is not surprising to find that the women in LeClézio's books are often found close to water. Chancelade and Adam both make advances to girls on the beach, and both fail to understand them. In *The Book of Flights* a woman is identified with a river; in *The Giants* Tranquilité and her friend drown; and finally NajaNaja walks on the water into the sunset, thus linking both images and providing an absolute contrast to François Besson crawling out to the end of the breakwater at the height of the storm. Besson seems to be trying to escape from his life and from the sort of relations with women where his security is constantly threatened; indeed, he is attempting to return to the womb. NajaNaja is the total opposite to the struggling image of rejection offered by Besson. She controls her environment; she has mystery, youth, beauty, flexibility, competence; she commands love and allegiance and seems to have power over all of life and death. LeClézio gives her the attributes of the archetypal woman. As we have seen earlier, she is linked to the sea and also to water in the form of Light Rain. In the conversation quoted above, LeClézio gives his definition of water as knowledge of yourself and of the reasons for life itself. The proximity of women (particularly in sexual situations) to the sea, the scene between Chancelade and his son on the beach, and NajaNaja's storytelling sessions there also take on clear meaning in this context, as does Tranquilité's watery suicide and the drowning in *The Interrogation*. Adam Pollo's gesture of throwing his motorbike into the sea to make people believe he has drowned simultaneously reveals the game Pollo is playing with himself and the process of comprehension.

A point of additional interest arises when we look at the context of LeClézio's statement about water. He is telling a story from Panama:

P. Lhoste: In Panama there is a tree you admire a great deal. . . .
LeClézio: Yes, it's the tree of Cuippó, it's the magic tree above all others. It gave water to men. One day, seeing this tree, men committed the sacrilegious act of cutting it down. The tree fell and the roots gave streams, the trunk gave rivers, and the branches gave the sea.[2]

The tree is full of water, hence the knowledge of life gained from water comes originally from a tree. NajaNaja, in one of her first attempts to teach her friends the other side of things, tries to make them enter into trees. And Adam raped Michèle under a tree in the rain, a scene in which the language reminds us of the Garden of Eden and the Fall. Hence we have come full circle to the Tree of Knowledge and the Tree of Life, to the situation where woman is both Eve (Michèle) and the Serpent (NajaNaja) and where man is tossed out into a hostile world through which he is destined to flee in search of his lost Paradise. The archetypal burdens of solitude and flight are faced by LeClézio's heroes.

II *Influences*

Solitude, alienation from society, its people and values, and travel in Asia and South and Central America where alternative philosophies can be found have brought LeClézio along a path very similar to the one he traced in the work of Henri Michaux at the time when his own body of work was embryonic. The cohesion that exists between LeClézio's critical work and his creative writing is striking. Everywhere we find the same choice, war or flight, imposed by a fundamental isolation rooted in fear; this is shared by Lautréamont, Artaud, and Michaux, to whom, as we have seen, LeClézio is drawn. For all of them writing is a safety valve protecting them more or less effectively from madness. Drugs and travel are used as means of escape and revelation. Each writer is concerned with the expression of his own deep feelings and his need to communicate them to others. This need for communication creates a profound struggle in the writers, owing to each one's alienation from his fellows, and produces a language of unusual violence coupled with a certain hermeticism. Writing is a second birth as traumatic as the first.

III *Language*

In an interview with Claudine Jardin in 1975, LeClézio states:

The most dramatic and marvellous moment in life is that second birth when one is born to language.

The earthly experience is first the adventure of man leaving the unexpressed universe in the direction of the world of language, then the recognition of the infinity of this language, its magnitude, its incompletion. Then words are no longer only those of speech (illusory and factitious indeed), but signs that life sends at him increasingly from all sides, appeals, orders, questions which are born of the sea, the sky, the earth, those words sometimes very slow and very long which murmur throughout a whole lifetime, those words sometimes so quick and sharp that they reach you without your perceiving them.

Finally the experience draws to an end into silence, and it is not the language which is extinguished but simply man's ear which ceases to perceive it. If man's language follows this apparent cycle from life to death, it is because it is precisely the most material, the most earthly of the adventures, blood, life. . . .

By words we go beyond words, we bring to life what the gaze alone cannot see. I think the adventure of language is beautiful because it makes us recognize roots, those which hold the world in position.[3]

The drama of birth into language is discussed at length by LeClézio in a review of Louis Wolfson's book *Le Schizo et les langues (The Schizo and Languages)*.[4] In the review he gives an interpretation of the role and function of language which throws light on the way he uses and presents language in his own work. As we realize clearly in *The Giants* if not before, words are part of the society in which we live and transmit its values not only by what they say but how they say it. LeClézio writes:

. . . accession to the world of language is not a simple phenomenon of adaptation with a view to communication. It is the first effort of man with regard to society, and thereby the source of his first pain, his first hatred. It is much less a question of speaking (to say what when it comes down to it?) than of entering the lists, of occupying the first square of the despairing and inevitable game of the contest.

. . . If language has become the very symbol of that struggle between the individual and society for him [Wolfson], it is because it was a deep expression of it. But the competiton is there, around him all the time. Competition in the family, competition at school, sexual competition. Besides he is particularly sensitive to all forms of organized competition, like examinations. . . . Indeed, language is itself a competition whose prizes are apparently distributed by chance: fortune, virility, success, happiness.

To accede to language is therefore to assure yourself of material comfort. It is to accept the rules of society, its injustices, and to try and turn them to your profit. (143–144)

Here we see the problem which faces any writer in revolt against society. His very means of expression belongs to the system he wishes to attack and thus must be dislocated, transformed before he can achieve his end. LeClézio's ambiguous relationship to language which creates outbursts against writers and writing which he writes down nonetheless begin to look less like fatuous fulminations. There is a real struggle going on between the individual and society which is defined here. On the one hand: "The language of others (that is his mother's) is a sort of permanent rape for him, an aggression mounted against him to empty him of his substance," (144) against which the only protection is not to listen, not to talk. On the other, "There are no other means of having access to consciousness except through language." (145) The solution lies in the act of writing because, "Transformed into writing, destined for publication, it [language] enters so to speak the sovereign domain of books, libraries, culture, and it ceases to be betrayal in order to become a subject of study, end and means—and perhaps, by its plenitude, a remedy for the crack and a way to a cure." There is a distance between the writer and his reader which does not exist in verbal exchange. Written language can be worked over again and again until the writer is sure that he has expressed only and exactly the amount he wishes to reveal. There is less fear of inadvertant self-betrayal and yet the desired contact with others exists for ". . . language is immediately conceived of as a social, physical act, whose acceptance is as indispensable to the body as food, drink, defecation and coitus." (147)

Writing is therefore an indirect means of being accepted by society by one who suffers from a feeling of rejection. But, as we have stated above, the act of self-expression is a violent and painful one for such authors. Not only that but their reactions toward those to whom they are alien vacillate between hatred and revolt and the need to be accepted. The result is usually tormented, violent, raw. It calls into question the whole of accepted literature: "The book becomes a kind of implacable, solitary avenger who destroys at one blow years of habits and literary comfort." (139)

Granted we are dealing, at present, with a review of someone else's work—with an author who is a true schizophrenic with very, very extreme reactions to language (he invents his own from foreign languages he has learned); but LeClézio brings the discussion closer to himself by comparing Wolfson's book to the work of Lautréamont and Michaux:

and what are the *Songs of Maldoror*, for example or *The Parisian Peasant*, or Michaux's poems? . . . A quivering book, alive, at the same time extraordinarily ferocious and tender, which imposes its own logic, which establishes its solitary language, which works at the elaboration of its own universe, for itself alone, according to this monstrous and inevitable egocentricity which is the very nature of thought. A book, the book *par excellence*, for there is no distance between what it says and the person who wrote it. The one and the other are part of the same whole. (15)

When the author coincides with his work in one and the same language then an important event has occurred for we are shaken out of our habits and forced to consider what LeClézio calls "the danger of speech, its urgency, its suffering." This is what he has been trying to do himself throughout his work. Once again his criticism proves our best tool in regard to himself. We find his theme and even one of his recurrent images in his description of Wolfson's situation: "A corrupt, greedy society full of appetites and illogicality where he is the only one to have understood what is going on. In his new society, he has invented a new language, could we say an antiseptic language. Each word, exploded, transformed, reconstructed according to a personal logic is like an antibody which fights against illness./This hermetic domain of language, this secret code is the search for affirmation of self in the face of the incoherence of other people." (149)

Fact in the case of Wolfson, metaphor in the case of LeClézio, the description is of language wielded as both a weapon, a shield, and an instrument of discovery. In his final sentences LeClézio takes a stand with Wolfson, Michaux, and the others to state the real function of books, the affirmation of which can be found throughout his own work: ". . . there are no beautiful books nor art books. There are only interesting books. There are only useful books. For it is doubtless the great discovery of our time to have rooted us out of peace toward doubt and misfortune, torn us away from the calm language which knew how to tell lies well and to have shown us, to show us everyday, with a little more pain and consciousness, that language is not a harmony but an explosion, that literature must no longer be made by one but by all." (151–152)

IV *Technique*

That LeClézio's struggle is a personal one manifests itself, in the early novels at least, by the fact that his characters are very alike and that each of the young men is similar in a number of respects to LeClézio himself. They are all alternative statements of the same thing. Indeed, the juxtaposition of alternatives is a technique the author uses at all levels and, in particular, we have noted the instability of his subject pronouns at all times. Narration moves frequently from "I" to "you" to "he" without any apparent motivation—a technique which both alienates the reader and forces him to share the alienation of narrator and protagonist very intimately. The novels have little or no plot, and in many cases the sections within a book have no apparent order. Usually they are made up of a series of situations which illustrate a given theme from different angles. These can be complementary or contradictory, developing the theme further or offering another possibility, a different interpretation. The effect is that of a number of tableaux rather than of continuous narration. Each book is complete in itself and yet is linked to the other works by a system of recurrent detail, repetition of images, new or further treatment of themes and problems. Hence all LeClézio's writings are woven together into a single growing structure in which each strand reinforces the others, and adds to their combined impact and power.

The resulting form with its facets of possibility recalls that of medieval narrative rather than any of the more recent techniques which tend to demand a single "true" version of a given event. The description which fits LeClézio's method most nearly is one given by Eugène Vinaver in a very different context. In his book, *In Search of a Theory of Mediaeval Poetry*,[5] Professor Vinaver writes: "One adventure prolongs another which was started a long time ago, takes up again or recalls something else that has already happened. No beginning in the true sense of the word, nothing but a succession of restarts, a group of themes which are always in motion and which are developed in turn. . . ."[6] The quotation refers to the tales of Arthur and the Knights of the Round Table, the ultimate collection of journeys and false starts centered around a singleminded quest for understanding, purity, and peace. What could be more fitting than to apply it to a struggle against the corruptions of modern society?

Against society LeClézio pits the forces of the natural world, and, above all, the elements. He is a relentless observer of the world around him, with the patience to record minute details, long sequences of phenomena, actions, and the gift to transpose what he has seen into words with extraordinary realism. It has been suggested that his evocations of heat are the most telling in the whole of French literature, and it is certainly true that he excels in the creation of "set-piece" descriptions: a storm at sea, a rainy night, and so on. His books are permeated by atmospheric conditions, overwhelmed by consumer goods and modern building. This is his universe. The only objection that can be made is that sometimes the author seems to be fascinated by the flow of his own sentences, and his effects then lack a conciseness which would increase their force.

In his personal explorations he has pushed beyond the usually accepted bounds of the novel into a realm of lyric reflection in which fiction, philosophy, and poetry are combined. It is no wonder that frequent references are found to pre-Socratic philosophers both in LeClézio's writing and that of his critics. Like them LeClézio is trying to describe the universe, and his cosmic prefaces and epilogues are but the more extreme of his attempts.

In many ways he reminds us of Jean-Jacques Rousseau. Both are intensely personal writers, consummate stylists, mystics making pertinent social criticisms, observers of nature in all its forms. Both reveal acute problems in their personal relations with other people and with women in particular. It is partly the result of each one's need to be accepted that they write copiously.

Given these resemblances, it would seem proper to end this study with two well-known quotations from Rousseau. LeClézio's treatment of these statements is very different from that of his predecessor, but the criticisms contained in them sum up his attitude very well: "Man is born free and everywhere he is in chains." "Everything is good when it comes from the hands of the author of all things; everything degenerates in the hands of man." LeClézio indicts modern society, its growth and values, and shares with us his attempts to resist its pressures. He sees life as a period of uncertainty, movement, change between birth and death which both lead out into darkness. His is a totally relative universe where particles swirl, combining and dividing in a constant shift, and where matter may assemble in the shape of man for a short time—this is the result of modern science. Simultaneously, LeClézio is a humanist of sorts. He believes that man, thus formed, should take responsibility for his context. He should remain as closely tied as possible to the other natural formations around him, for through them he can come to know himself perhaps. The man-made elements of the modern world prevent him from doing this—they alienate him from matter and therefore from himself, who is matter also. LeClézio's work is one long attempt to deal with alienation and the accompanying diminution of the individual. By his way of writing he forces us to share and come to grips with his situation and therefore our own. He is a man of our time, and his writing is a valuable addition to the corpus of available experience.

Notes and References

Chapter Two

1. In the references to quotations from LeClézio's works, the first page number following each quotation is to the English translation listed in the bibliography, the second, prefixed by "G" to the Gallimard first edition.
2. Interview with Jean-Louis de Rambures, *Le Monde* September 5th, 1970.

Chapter Three

1. Jean-Louis Bory, "Neuf bateaux ivres," *Le Nouvel Observateur* March 25th, 1965, p. 24.
2. *Les Nouvelles Littéraires* July 10th, 1969.
3. Georges Bortoli, "Rien n'a changé pour LeClézio," *Le Figaro Littéraire* no. 965, October 15th, 1964, p.3.
4. Ibid.

Chapter Four

1. Robert Kanters, "LeClézio à la recherche de l'Arche," *Le Figaro Littéraire* March 17th, 1966, p. 5.
2. This reminds us of Josette. See p. 106 G106.
3. *Combat* March 12th–13th, 1969, p. 9.

Chapter Five

1. Alan W. Watts, *Psychotherapy East and West* (London: Penguin 1973), p. 42.
2. Tao Te Ching 2.
3. D. T. Suzuki, *Zen and Japanese Culture* (New York: Pantheon 1959), p. 353.
4. *Hsin-hsin ming*, in *The Way of Zen* by A. W. Watts (London: Thames and Hudson 1957), p. 115.
5. See Chapter 12: Influences.

Chapter Six

1. *L'Express* November 21st, 1963, p. 31.
2. See 169 G190.

3. P. Kyria, "J. M. G. LeClézio, three years afterwards," *Combat* March 12th–13th, 1966, p. 9.

4. There is a sentence missing in the translation. The French text reads ". . .archaeology. I could have gone into space, or read philosophy books. I might have had. . ."

Chapter Seven

1. *Le Monde* May 24th, 1969.
2. Ibid.
3. This is quoted from the *Isa Upanisad.*

Chapter Nine

1. No. 17 January 1973. A second publication "Le jardin aux serpents" (The Snake Garden) *Les Cahiers du chemin* no. 18, April 1973 might also be part of *Au Pays d'Iwa.*
2. *Les Nouvelles Littéraires* July 10th, 1969, p. 11.
3. *Les Nouvelles Littéraires* October 29th, 1970, p. 7.

Chapter Ten

1. As the English version of *The Giants* appeared after my work was finished all translations in this chapter are my own, and no page reference is given to the translation.
2. The name is given as EGGS in the French text, hence I have used the French word in my translation to obtain the same effect.

Chapter Eleven

1. No translation of *Voyages de l'autre côté* exists at present. All translations are therefore my own.
2. Both references are taken from M. Butor, *Portrait de l'artiste en jeune singe* (Paris: Gallimard 1967).
3. *Le Figaro Littéraire* February 9th, 1975, p. 5.
4. Ibid.
5. *Terra Amata* 144 G162–3.
6. *Les Cahiers du chemin* no. 18 (Paris: Gallimard 1973), p. 62.
7. *Le Figaro Littéraire* February 9th, 1975, p. 5.
8. Ibid., p. 6.

Chapter Twelve

1. A copy is available for consultation in the University library in Nice. All page references are to this copy.
2. In his thesis LeClézio incorporates bibliographical references into the body of the text, hence when quoting passages from it I have made no change in style.
3. R. Bertelé *Michaux* (Paris: P. Seghers 1957), p. 13 quoted by LeClézio, p. 34.

4. *Les Cahiers du chemin* no. 13 October 15th, 1971. All references to this review will be abbreviated to *Cahiers*.

5. *Lautréamont, Entretiens* no. 30 (Rodez: Editions Supervie 1971). This critical collection will be referred to as *Lautréamont* in the future.

6. Lautréamont, *Oeuvres Complètes* (Paris: Gallimard, Collection Poésie, 1973). All further references will be to *Oeuvres*.

7. *Cahiers* p. 104.

8. Ibid. p. 118.

9. *Oeuvres* p. 12.

10. *Cahiers* p. 108.

11. Ibid. p. 118.

12. *Oeuvres* p. 9.

13. *Cahiers* p. 120.

14. *Oeuvres* p. 14.

15. "L'Envoûté," *Les Cahiers du chemin* no. 19, October 15th, 1973. All page references in section III are to this article.

Chapter Thirteen

1. *Conversations avec LeClézio* (Paris: Mercure de France 1971), pp. 123–124.

2. Ibid. p. 123.

3. *Le Figaro Littéraire* February 9th, 1975, p. 6.

4. *Les Cahiers du chemin* no. 10, October 15th, 1970, pp. 139–152. All subsequent page references in section III refer to this review.

5. Nizet 1970.

6. Ibid. p. 159.

Selected Bibliography

PRIMARY SOURCES

1. Fiction and Essays

Le Procès-verbal. Paris: Gallimard, 1963. Winner of the Prix Renaudot.
Le jour où Beaumont fit connaissance avec sa douleur. Paris: Mercure de
    France, 1964.
La Fièvre. Paris: Gallimard, 1965.
L'Extase matérielle. Paris: Gallimard, 1966.
Le Déluge. Paris: Gallimard, 1968.
Terra Amata. Paris: Gallimard, 1968.
Le Livre des fuites. Paris: Gallimard, 1969.
La Guerre. Paris: Gallimard, 1970.
Haï. Collection Les Sentiers de la Création, Geneva: Skira, 1971.
Mydriase. Montpellier: Fata Morgana, 1973.
Les Géants. Paris: Gallimard, 1973.
Voyages de l'autre côté. Paris: Gallimard, 1975.

2. Stories and Descriptive texts

"L'Extra-terrestre." *Fellini, L'Arc* no. 45 (1971), pp. 27–29.
"Histoire du château qui explosait et renaissait sans cesse." *La Nouvelle
    Revue Française*, no. 221 (May, 1971), pp. 69–79.
"Le Génie Datura." *Les Cahiers du chemin*, no. 17 (January 15, 1973), pp.
    95–129.
"Trois villes saintes." *La Nouvelle Revue Française*, no. 264 (December,
    1974), pp. 1–15 and 273 (September, 1975), pp. 7–33.
Contributions to *Les Cahiers du Chemin*, nos. 2, 5, 7, 9, 10, 12, 13, 15, 18,
    22, 23 and *La Nouvelle Revue Française*, no. 262. Most of these are
    extracts from subsequently published works.

3. Literary Criticism

"Sur Henri Michaux, Fragments," *Les Cahiers du Sud*, no. 380 (1964),
    pp. 262–69.

173

Preface to *Et ce sont les violents qui l'emportent* by Flannery O'Connor (Paris: Gallimard, 1965), pp. 7–13.

"Un homme exemplaire," in *Jean Paul Sartre, L'Arc* no. 30 (1966), pp. 5–9.

"Sartre par LeClézio," in *L'Express* no. 801 (October 24–30, 1966), pp. 35–36.

Review of *Le Schizo et les langues* by Louis Wolfson. *Les Cahiers du chemin*, no. 10 (October 15, 1970), pp. 139–52.

"L'autre est Lautréamont," in *Lautréamont, Entretiens* no. 30 (Rodez: Editions Supervie 1971), pp. 153–58.

"L'envoûté (Artaud)," *Les Cahiers du chemin* no. 19 (October 15, 1973, pp. 51–67.

Preface to *Oeuvres Complètes, Les Chants de Maldoror, Lettres, Poésies I et II* by Isidore Ducasse, Comte de Lautréamont (Paris: NRF, Gallimard 1973), pp. 7–14.

"Un poème (Iniji) qui n'est pas comme les autres," *La Quinzaine Littéraire* (July 16–31, 1973), pp. 5–7.

4. Translations

The Interrogation. Translated by Daphne Woodward. London: Hamish Hamilton, 1964.

Fever. Translated by Daphne Woodward. New York: Atheneum, 1966.

The Flood. Translated by Peter Green. New York: Atheneum, 1968.

Terra Amata. Translated by Barbara Bray. London: Hamish Hamilton, 1969.

The Book of Flights. Translated by Simon Watson Taylor. New York: Atheneum, 1972.

War. Translated by Simon Watson Taylor. London: Johnathon Cape and Wildwood House, 1973.

The Giants. Translated by Simon Watson Taylor. New York: Atheneum, 1975.

5. Interviews

LHOSTE, PIERRE. *Conversations avec J. M. G. LeClézio.* Paris: Mercure de France, 1971. Wide Ranging discussions. Interesting and informative.

ALBO, DANIEL. "LeClézio 'prof' de français à Bangkok," *Le Figaro Littéraire*, May 2, 1967, pp. 26–27. Biographical material.

BORTOLI, GEORGES. "Rien n'a changé pour LeClézio," *Le Figaro Littéraire*, October 15, 1964, p.3. Interesting on characters and the author's relationship to them and to society.

CHALON, JEAN. "J. M. G. LeClézio, philosophe de 23 ans avoue 'Je suis paresseux,'" *Le Figaro Littéraire*, November 21, 1963, p. 3. Discussion of his life and philosophy at the time of his Prix Renaudot.

CHAPSAL, MADELEINE. "Un poème inédit de J. M. G. LeClézio," *L'Express* no. 649, November 21, 1963, pp. 31–32. An attempt to learn what has influenced him. LeClézio is evasive.

―――. "LeClézio rentre d'Amérique," *L'Express*, August 2, 1965, pp. 36–37. Comments on America.

DAIX, PIERRE. "Avec LeClézio," *Les Lettres Françaises*, July 30, 1964, pp. 1:7. Surrealism, Michaux and *The Interrogation*. Useful.

DELPECHE, JANINE. "LeClézio: La paresse récompensée," *Les Nouvelles Littéraires*, November 21, 1963, pp. 1:6. Authors LeClézio read and liked.

MOURTHE, CLAUDE et al. "LeClézio a réponse à tous," *Le Figaro Littéraire*, February 9, 1975, pp. 5–6. Fascinating discussion of the sun and solitude, rebirth and language.

KYRIA, PIERRE. "J. M. G. LeCézio trois ans après," *Combat* March 12–13, 1966, p. 9. On God, *The Flood* and reasons for writing.

LHOSTE, PIERRE. "Entretien avec J. M. G. LeClézio," *Les Nouvelles Littéraires*, July 19, 1969, pp. 1:11. Very interesting interview starting from *The Flood*.

―――. "Je fuis l'Europe des esclaves," *Les Nouvelles Littéraires*, October 29, 1970, pp. 1:7. Equally interesting. Both are thematic and similar to *Conversations*.

RAMBURES JEAN-LOUIS DE. "J'écris pour ne pas rêver, pour ne pas souffrir," *Le Monde*, September 5, 1970. Work methods and *The Book of Flights*.

SECONDARY SOURCES

See *French XX Bibliography*, New York: French Institute-Alliance Française and The Camargo Foundation (published annually) for further studies.

1. Article length studies

ALBÉRÈS, RENE MARIL. *Littérature horizon 2000*. Paris: Albin Michel 1973, pp. 179–99. Brief analysis of "cosmic" writing. Interesting.

ANON. "Le poète de la peur de vivre: LeClézio," *Réalités*, March 1967, pp. 101–11. Perspicacious comments on *The Interrogation*.

BERSANI, JACQUES. "LeClézio sismographe," *Critique*, XX. 238 (March 1967), pp. 311–21. Good criticism of *The Interrogation. Fever* and *The Flood*.

―――. "Sagesse de LeClézio," *La Nouvelle Revue Française*, XV-175 (July 1, 1967), pp. 110–15. Useful review of *L'Extase matérielle*.

BOLLEME, GENEVIEVE. "Le Procès-verbal ou la folie fiction," *Mercure de France*, XII (December 1973), pp. 791–97. Comparison of the style and tone of *The Interrogation* to that of Giraudoux's novels.

BUREAU, CONRAD. *Linguistique fonctionnelle et stylistique objective*. Paris: Presses Universitaires de France 1976. Detailed study of LeClézio's style.

CAGNON, MAURICE. "J. M. G. LeClézio, l'impossible vérité de la fiction," *Critique*, no. 297 (February 1972), pp. 158–64. *The Book of Flights*.

Dialectic between movement and rest, multiplicity and unity, reality and imagination.

———. "J. M. G. LeClézio, The Genesis of Writing," *Language and Style*, V3 (Summer 1972), pp. 221–27. Detailed comparison of "Comment j'écris" and *The Book of Flights* showing the shift from one text to another.

CAGNON, MAURICE and STEPHEN SMITH "LeClézio's Taoist vision," *French Review* XLVII special issue no. 6 (Spring 1974), pp. 245–52. On Oriental influences.

———. "Mors et anima: la Dialectique du Paradoxe Plausible," *Revue du Pacifique*, I no. 1 (Spring 1975), pp. 33–42. A splendid paper which reveals the patterned complexity of LeClézio's world.

———. "J. M. G. LeClézio: Fiction's Double Bind" in Raymond Federman, ed., *Surfiction: Fiction Today and Tomorrow*, Chicago: Swallow Press. 1975.

JEAN, RAYMOND. "L'Univers biologique de J. M. G. LeClézio," *Cahiers du Sud*, LIX, 382 (May 1965), pp. 285–88. Interesting discussion of the physical reactions in *Fever*.

———. *La Littérature et le réel*. Paris: Albin Michel 1965. One good chapter on LeClézio.

KANTERS, ROBERT. "Jean-Marie Gustave LeClézio" in *L'Air des Lettres*, Paris: Grasset 1973, pp. 492–503. Three brief analyses: Adam Pollo, *L'Extase matérielle* and *War*.

MOREAU, PIERRE. "Le moi et le sentiment de l'existence dans la littérature française contemporaine," *Archives des Lettres Modernes* no. 147 (1973), pp. 9–66. A comparative work with multiple brief references to LeClézio.

REVEL, JEAN-FRANÇOIS. "La Rolls du Clézio," in *Les Idées de Notre Temps*. Paris: Laffont, 1972, pp. 90–92. A negative review of *L'Extase matérielle*.

SIMON, PIERRE-HENRI. *Parier pour l'homme*. Paris: Seuil 1973, pp. 303–13. Reviews of *Fever* and *L'Extase matérielle* which consider the qualities of LeClézio's prose.

ZELTNER, GERDA. "Jean-Marie Gustave LeClézio: Le Roman Antiformaliste," *Positions et Oppositions sur le Roman Contemporain*, Actes et Colloques no. 8, edited by Michel Mansuy. Strasbourg: Editions Klincksieck, 1971, pp. 215–28. LeClézio in context: his vision in *The Interrogation vis à vis* that of other modern writers, especially the *nouveaux romanciers*.

2 Dissertations

BOTTGEN, JEAN-PAUL. "Etude thématique de *La Fièvre* de J. M. G. LeClézio: pour un mythe du réel chez J. M. G. LeClézio." Master's dissertation. University of Nice 1972. An extremely detailed study of *Fever*.

CHEZET, JEAN-PAUL DE. "Continuité et discontinuité dans les romans de J. M. G. LeClézio." PhD dissertation, University of California, Irvine, 1974. An excellent analysis of all the books from *The Interrogation* to *The Giants*.

DAROS, PHILIPPE. "L'Oeuvre: Expérience de la déraison: Etude du *Procès-verbal* et d'autres textes de J. M. G. LeClézio." Master's dissertation. University of Nice, 1973. More a study of modern critical apparatus than of LeClézio.

MAISONNEUVE, PATRICK. "L'univers mythologique du roman français contemporain d'Alain Robbe-Grillet à J. M. G. LeClézio." Doctorat du 3e cycle, University of Paris VIII, 1971, Interesting comparisons.

REILAND, ALAIN. "Les romans de J. M. G. LeClézio. Structures imaginaires, structures romanesques." Master's disseration. University of Strasbourg, 1972. An interesting study of the early writing.

REISH, KATHLEEN WHITE. "J. M. G. LeClézio. The building of a fictional world." PhD dissertation, University of Wisconsin, 1973. A very useful work covering the period from *The Interrogation to War*.

SALIJ, H. J. "Modern dilemmas and the techniques of writing in the novels of Uwe Johnson and J. M. G. LeClézio." PhD dissertation, University of Washington, 1971. Excellent commentary on style and narrative technique.

Index